LIVING IN STORMS

EASTERN WASHINGTON UNIVERSITY PRESS

LIVING IN STORMS

contemporary poetry and the moods of manic-depression

edited by Thom Schramm

Cover art: Gary Isaacs, *Woman Dancing in Meadow*. Used by permission.

Design and typography by A. E. Grey

Library of Congress Cataloging-in-Publication Data

Living in storms : contemporary poetry and the moods of manic-depression /
edited by Thom Schramm.
    p.   cm.
  Includes bibliographical references and index.
  ISBN 978-1-59766-031-0 (alk. paper)
  1. American poetry—21st century. 2. Manic-depressive illness—Poetry. I.
Schramm, Thom.
PS617.L58 2007
811'.6080353—dc22

                                                          2007035618

Eastern Washington University Press

Spokane and Cheney, Washington

For my parents
and
in memoriam, Jane Kenyon (1947–1995)

CONTENTS

REMEMBERING THE EPISODES

CHARACTERS

FRIENDS AND FAMILY

THE ARTIST

"Happiness writes white," says Philip Larkin in a famous interview, quoting Henry de Montherlant. "It's very difficult to write about being happy. Very easy to write about being miserable. And I think writing about unhappiness is the source of my popularity, if I have any—after all, most people *are* unhappy, don't you think?" It is hard to argue with such epigrammatic certainty, but even Larkin, if pressed, would probably have admitted that the issue is not so simple. True, odes to dejection, despair, and our manifold variants on brooding seem very common in lyric poetry, much more common than odes to joy, or even to simple well-being. But Larkin, that most painstaking of craftsmen, knew that despair as well seems often to write white, and this is not surprising. The emotional agents that drive us to poetry are difficult to understand, let alone to master, and herein lies a paradox that continually afflicts all serious poets: the composition of verse is an act of will, but in several crucial ways it is also a hugely mysterious process. Given these complexities, it *should be* impossible for any of us to write good poetry, for, on the one hand, we will never be able to fully command verse craft, its music and language; and, on the other, we will never possess the wisdom that would permit us to truly know ourselves. Poetry exists somewhere within this causal chain of paradoxes that Keats described as Negative Capability.

One of the most perplexing of these mysteries and paradoxes is that poets are often inspired by emotional states that are in almost every way difficult for the poet to tolerate. No one likes to suffer from depression, and the enthralled sense of power and the sourceless joy that accompany the initial stages of mania are also difficult to bear, for they will sooner or later wear off, replaced by the dreariest forms of abjection. Happiness or sadness? Happiness *versus* sadness? It is of course more mysterious and complex than this, as the poets in this anthology know.

Such mysteries may be related in part to the chemical composition of the brain, as the poets in this anthology no doubt also understand—for this is the first anthology of poetry explicitly and exclusively to choose as its subject bipolar disorder. In recent years experts have come to see that this disorder, which is also termed manic-depression and is known in its milder form as cyclothymia, affects millions of Americans, and some say it strikes artists, writers, and composers with disproportionate frequency. The list of creative artists afflicted is said to go well beyond the familiar roll call of mad British poets represented by William Cowper, Christopher Smart, and John Clare (among others) or the tortured American middle generation poets such as Robert Lowell, John Berryman, Anne Sexton, Sylvia Plath, Elizabeth Bishop, and Randall Jarrell.

The statistics are sobering, but statistics should not be confused with the Muse, even when the Muse asks us to sing the most melancholy blues. Poetry speaks from the conditions that produce it, but good poetry doesn't do *merely* that. This anthology is notable mainly for the striking and powerful poems it contains, which represent a wide range of responses to a particular adversity. Many of the poems of course focus on the self and its struggles with mania and depression, but others describe the impact of the disorder on friends and family members, while still others are homages to earlier artists, writers, and composers afflicted with mania and depression. Thom Schramm has chosen his selections well. The poets represented here are remarkably disinclined to confessional self-indulgence and self-pity; they confront their conditions with a harrowing lucidity, and sometimes with a self-mocking humor. The portraits of friends and relatives who suffer from mania and depression are empathic and sharply observed. The vexing emotional swings and extremities characteristic of manic-depression are shown to us in an almost comprehensive fashion. All the cycles, all the inexplicable euphorias, and all the self-nullifying despairs are here—but so are the brave and tentative recoveries from such states.

The accomplishment of these poems is that they express, with dignity and grace, what Coleridge in his "Dejection" ode called "the eddying of [the] living soul." And this is what poems are meant to do.

—David Wojahn

INTRODUCTION

The moods characteristic of manic-depression resemble basic moods we all have felt. If a divorce causes deep sorrow, a sudden deadline inspires frantic activity, or thirty consecutive overcast days make us irritable, we know we are human. But why do some of us suffer more acute or more frequent moods than others? The earliest explanation alleged that spiritual possession caused thoughts and behavior amounting to mania. And Richard Burton's gigantic treatise *The Anatomy of Melancholy* (1621) listed countless natural and supernatural reasons why a seventeenth-century individual might have felt depressed, including unbalanced body fluids, bad habits, and a hot brain. Every major philosophical and medical development thereafter produced theories nearly as plentiful as Burton's.[1] Today, psychological and medical authorities variously attribute disorderly moods to trauma, repression, thought patterns learned in childhood, aberrant genes that cause neurotransmitter malfunction, environmental stress, poor nutrition, and the like. Abundantly documented, these rival definitions and etiologies reflect a fierce debate that epitomizes the nature versus nurture controversy and turns on the phrase "mental illness."

Undeniably, the language used to describe moods and define mental illness significantly determines the debate. Given that moods occur on a continuum that includes appropriate and beneficial emotional responses to stress, deciding exactly when an emotional state has become excessive requires reasonably precise language, subtle interpretation, and careful evaluation. Generally this is a thorny and indefinite undertaking. Attempting to eliminate the unreliability that theory-based methods such as psychoanalysis supposedly entail, the medical method delineates disorder using systematically derived, symptom-based criteria.[2] The process used to arrive at these criteria has been criticized on many grounds. Certain critics, among them sociologists and philosophers, argue that categories of mental disorder express a limited set of cultural values and are hence biased, a problem compounded by the fact that diagnostic criteria primarily address specific behaviors and emotions discretely, abstracted from the contexts that might generate or precipitate them.[3] Others maintain that it is a mistake to label undesirable moods symptoms of mental illness—a process that some think unwisely or wrongly interprets human emotions in medical terms, possibly to justify social control.[4] Within this contentious environment, some of the theorists who try to distinguish between healthy and unhealthy moods have hypothesized that a propensity to experience acute moods confers evolutionary advantages. This approach drifts into another wide-ranging debate concerning the relationship between so-called madness and creativity—a term also difficult to define.[5] Is there such a relationship? And, if so, is it a cause-and-effect relationship?

Poets periodically star in these ancient arguments. Plato had it that they are endowed with divine madness,[6] a view all but confirmed centuries later by Romantic poets who led famously inspired lives, occasionally inside state-of-the-art asylums. And the public spectacle of Sylvia Plath's and Anne Sexton's suicides extended the legendary image of the mad poet into modern consciousness. Before long, researchers took to examining poets and usually concluded that their feelings and behavior met diagnostic criteria for mood disorders proportionally more than did those of other groups. A well-known 1987 study by Nancy Andreasen, based on interviews she conducted at the Iowa Writers' Workshop, found that an exceptionally high percentage of her sample of thirty writers (presumably including poets) had experienced symptoms of manic-depression.[7] Several years later, Kay Jamison's popular book, *Touched with Fire: Manic-Depressive Illness and the Artistic Temperament* (1993), surveyed the turbulent lives of numerous poets (none still living) and examined their writing through the lens of illness.[8] In another noted book, *The Price of Greatness* (1995), Arnold Ludwig scrutinized the biographies of a large number of eminent creative individuals and claimed that poets were especially likely to have experienced a mood disorder.[9] These researchers all alleged that a positive correlation exists between mental disorder and creativity, although they differed in their assessments of the degree to which disorder might contribute to creativity. Dissenting from their broadly accepted conclusions, Albert Rothenberg has sharply criticized the methodology of influential studies that associate creativity and mood disorders, contending instead—based on evidence gathered from his own psychiatric interviews and psychological experiments—that creativity calls for mental health.[10] Nonscientific works that discuss the moods of poets include biographies of Emily Dickinson, Vachel Lindsay, Theodore Roethke, Delmore Schwartz, John Berryman, Randall Jarrell, Anne Sexton, Robert Lowell, and Sylvia Plath, all of which describe the manic and depressive episodes these poets suffered.[11]

Initially, most of these works would seem to validate the familiar "mad poet" stereotype. However, they contain crucial defects. Perhaps inevitably, the nonscientific works tend inappropriately to invoke diagnostic terms best applied only after rigorous clinical assessment. More importantly, the relatively few systematic studies that might appear to offer support for a link between mood disorders and creativity, and on which popular authors and researchers have repeatedly relied, are marred by weak design. Among their weaknesses are inconsistent definitions both of mental disorder and of creativity, the psychological assessment of writers solely on the basis of biographical material or "non-blind" interviews, and the lack of proper control groups.[12] Findings from such inherently flawed studies can hardly confirm an essential connection between mood disorders and creativity. Nevertheless, in conjunction with a well-developed mystique and widely chronicled suicides, they have advanced a skewed impression of poets and of the demands of creativity. The stereotype persists partly because the literature generally overlooks the intricate details and contexts of individual lives—the fact that no two people suffer depression or mania in precisely the same way.

Poems counterbalance such literature. For centuries poets have contemplated and portrayed moods, and, although but a small fraction of all poetry, numerous poems make moods their central concern. Some even contain the terms *manic-depression* or *bipolar* (as the disorder has come metaphorically to be called). Yet poems generously accommodate imagination and affecting language. They specify assorted species of mood, as well as their occasions and locations. For instance, in "Returning from the Shopping Center to the Suburbs," Peter Cooley remarks almost offhandedly: "It's hard / to get ahead these days; you know, / while your soul keeps panting up behind you." After he impulsively lets go of the steering wheel, a car he faces head-on swerves, missing him, and he convinces himself, "I'm among the chosen"—but then shifts and ends insecurely, with a challenge: "How do you get through your life?" Elsewhere a field fills with natural symbols that seem inexplicably to inflame emotion: the forsythia's "nitric yellow," in Brigit Kelly's "Figure of Distress in a Field," "shatters the thin air: the thin / Panes of spent denial and // Full the hurt comes down." The profuse field fills with action that evokes agitation and distress, and the figure of a crow provokes reflection on what Kelly calls "this bitterness // Of thought and its better brothers." Nuanced poems like these, whose curious, metaphoric methods bear emotion and unconventional associations, show us moods in their variable degrees and proportions.

This anthology's first sections—"How It Is," "In the Mood," and "Remembering the Episodes"—demonstrate the distinct ways poets depict and interpret depression and mania, at various distances from the immediate experience or apprehension of the mood. For example, in "Depressive," William Matthews wryly mimics depressive thinking when he claims, "It's work, / being depressed," and "the work of being / depressed is to stay depressed," an assertion that strikes to the very pith of misery. How devastating it feels when, after the line break, "being" meets "depressed"; existence itself is subjected, made passive by depression's repetitious labor. Given these circumstances, Matthews observes, "No wonder we love sad songs." In "Mania," what Susan Hahn bluntly calls "the bitch / part of me" is offset by a more expansive feeling:

> But when my brain swells
> and pushes on the small bones
> of my face, what spills out
> seems so rich. I think
> everyone loves me so much.

But eventually that generosity gives way, and she ends up "Hater of both halves / of myself—raving / slave, desperate dictator." Such extreme self-criticism exacerbates despair and begs for compassion, which Peter Meinke's poet refuses to grant himself: even God wants him to shut up, he believes ("The Poet to His Tongue"). The opposite pole is hyperconfidence, the "fully revved" feeling Daniel Halpern accesses—"amped-up and jagged with sound"—in "Rock Star Dream." Often these poems stage a confrontation. In "Having It Out with Melancholy," Jane Kenyon bravely eyes the demonlike persistence of moods that defy both the latest medical treatments and a friend's blaming suggestion: "You wouldn't be so depressed / if you really believed in God." Alane Rollings proposes, "Let's see what links events and moods"; then, brainstorming, she juxtaposes chaotic world events and private ones, volubly illustrating how they can collide with and infiltrate someone's consciousness, exposing "the logic of things in opposition" ("The Logic of Opposites").

Poems such as these exercise forms of poetic reasoning and powerfully illustrate language's potential to define and shape emotions and perceptions. When poets draw on images, metaphors, and symbols to describe a manic or depressive phase, they refigure the mood, rendering it specific and sensible, and they transform their perception of it into an aesthetic object that may move others—a healthy endeavor. Writing poetry can serve as an exorcism, and the poems themselves may, in turn, help their readers sustain or restore emotional balance. At the very least, when turmoil or gloom urges us toward verse, verse offers particular ways to order and fathom those states.

Nevertheless, artistry—more than therapeutic musing—demands special effort, and possibly special traits. Whether great artists acquire these mainly from upbringing or from biological disposition is a mystery that has inspired many studies of creativity, which inevitably consider whether "genius"—a quality usually ascribed to artists who have achieved eminence—presupposes pathology.[13] Complicating the genius status, though, is the fact that, besides individual psychology, social forces, and thus values and judgments, work to decide an artist's stature. The historical predilection for identifying poets as mad entails a bias that could influence which poets attain legitimacy or fame in a particular period—as in the Romantic period, for instance, when the impulse to ally genius and madness became something of a craze.[14]

Preconceptions also can corrupt research findings. Given the stereotype's tenacity, as well as the Romantic period's ongoing influence, observer bias—an overemphasis on expected behavior—could explain the stress that prominent studies have placed on the association between creativity and pathology, even though evidence also exists to demonstrate that artists possess exceptionally healthy psychological traits such as self-confidence, ego strength, and other abilities that creative achievement demands: flexible thinking, openness to experience, industriousness, and motivation.[15] It is especially difficult to reconcile these facts with the assertion that eminent artists are extraordinarily prone to emotional disorder.

Of course, a poet might exhibit symptoms only temporarily. But how exactly, and to what extent, such temporary states might influence or necessarily relate to a poet's creative achievement remains a highly contentious issue. One-time asylum resident Charles Lamb wrote, "The greatness of wit, by which the poetic talent is here chiefly to be understood, manifests itself in the admirable balance of all the faculties."[16] The fact is that seriously pursuing poetry requires vital, adaptive characteristics that poets manage to exploit despite possibly demanding moods and other, often extrinsic, obstacles. If necessary, a poet may objectify a trying mood, turn it into a nemesis, and project it into the world in an effort to make sense of, and combat, pain. David Ignatow demonstrates one way of coping:

> I must make my own sun
> regularly to avoid being
> lost within and frozen
> to death—the poem
> as I make it
> out of the wood
> of the forest where I wander
> rubbing the pieces together
> picked up
> as I stumble upon them.

Even if, pursuant to their art, they might deliberately engage intense feelings and conflicts and allow for unreason, many poets here appear to know they are handling mercury and to appreciate its value as well as its potential peril. Addressing William Blake, in "Epigraphs," Gerald Barrax declares, "If you are mad, Mr. Blake, /

it's not the poet in you: the sanest of men." But he goes on to admit that relinquishing a degree of rational control could be beneficial: "I'm nearly as willing to let my mind go a little, / to lean against the sun, / for one more poem."

While seriously practicing poetry can, on occasion, result in the kind of mental strain that could leave anyone vulnerable to a mood, that practice benefits from courage, intention, and will. Interestingly (if perhaps coincidentally), the word *mood* is derived from old Germanic words that meant these things, and some of the term's earliest meanings preserved these connotations.[17] Insofar as they drive ambition, these qualities serve a poet whose keen attention discerns and captures (or conjures) feelings and idiosyncratic thoughts that most people disregard or else do not reveal in the public way that poets do. Taken uncritically, this circumstance has led observers, including some poets, mistakenly to conclude that writing requires affliction and that disorder is poetry's sine qua non.[18] Such conclusions can seem reasonable when a reader confuses a poem with the person who wrote it and treats it strictly as nonfiction rather than as a work shaped by imagination. Inadvertently responding to Anne Sexton's view that "creative people must not avoid the pain that they get dealt" and that "hurt must be examined like a plague," Denise Levertov sensed a related hazard:

> To raise our fears and insecurities into consciousness in order to confront them, to deal with them, is good; but . . . if the pain is confused with art itself, then people at the receiving end of a poem describing a pain and insecurity they share are not really brought to confront and deal with their problems, but instead are led into a false acceptance of them as signs and precursors of art, marks of kinship with the admired artist, symptoms of what used to be called "the artistic temperament."[19]

The phrase "the artistic temperament" too conveniently reduces the various dispositions poets possess to one, implying that without that particular temperament a person cannot be an artist—that the artist must conform to certain societal expectations. But if an artistic temperament exists, poetically it would tend to express thought and emotion through a process ultimately unlike disorder. Wordsworth posits that "poetry is the spontaneous overflow of powerful feelings; it takes its origin from emotion recollected in tranquillity"[20]—emotion that he says poets contemplate and then strive to reconstitute. His famous theory neglects the hard work and skilled judgment necessary to create good poetry and encourages the fanciful view that unbidden inspiration is all a poet needs in order to write. And yet the tranquility and contemplative recollection that Wordsworth recognizes in fact imply poise, a state of mental equanimity that creative people can occupy quite consciously. Poise permits divergent associations and the synthesis of antithetical concepts—a manner of cognitive functioning that can look illogical and pathological but may actually be indicative of mental health, especially when it is integral to the creative process, as Rothenberg compellingly contends.[21]

Nonetheless, innumerable conditions impinge on creativity, including anxiety and inner conflict, and, lamentably, poets sometimes break down. But as Levertov insisted, "while the creative impulse and the self-destructive impulse can, and often do, coexist, their relationship is distinctly acausal; self-destructiveness is a handicap to the life of art, not the reverse."[22] William Stafford agreed:

> I don't feel that artists need to suffer. I don't think
> they can avoid it, but on the other hand, any kind
> of philosophy that would turn up the amount of
> suffering in order to improve the art seems to me
> a fantastic misreading of how organisms work. . . .
> I'm unconvinced by those who say that suffering
> results in creativity. No, no, creativity comes from
> a feeling of welcoming of impulses that come to
> you.[23]

Robert Mezey's measure of this wisdom is: "Nothing can so exhaust the heart / As boredom and self-loathing do, / Which are the poisons of my art" ("No Country You Remember").

The sections "Characters," "Friends and Family," and "The Artist" gather work by poets who stand as intermediaries between their readers and people in the throes of severe moods. From both firsthand knowledge and imagination, they model empathy and, in a sense, foster affiliation in cases where impenetrable isolation is the norm. That isolation is partly a function of moods themselves, but it can also be imposed by the stigma that accompanies mental disorder. Marjorie Power's "*The Madwoman* by Picasso" conveys the sense of disgrace that can haunt a person afflicted by severe depression: even the waves of the sea appear to shun the woman as they "avoid her place in the sand." When a man walks by, "He looks away fast," and she sees "the child / who stares in silence, / clutching a grown-up's hand." More sympathetic than the passerby who averts his gaze, Vern Rutsala imagines that the "darkness I know / but haven't seen" can touch us all: "We all know / it's there, know it waits." Pained by his inability to help a deeply depressed friend, he hopes in vain for a call, his own waiting a countervailing force against the darkness that lurks "in the closet beyond the closet / and in those canyons of ink / beneath our beds" ("Against Telephones"). In "Learning to Feed Ourselves," Carol Ann Borges starkly relates: "Momma had spells—what / else could you call them? / Seven days spent crying in bed." When that sort of episode occurred, her family would "just wait it out."

Calling such spells "major depression" or "bipolar depression" formulates them as medical problems, a circumstance that various poems in this collection highlight. Significantly, the medical model has prompted the development of drug treatments that help thwart the worst moods and chronic torments, as well as the impulse to commit suicide. For many people, a physician's diagnosis instigates change that leads eventually to increased stability. However, the line between necessary prescription and false cure remains blurry, and medical treatments still entail formidable philosophical and ethical problems, not to mention potentially serious side effects. Some treatments constrain people to an apparent behavioral norm but ignore the sources of their distress. Even sedated, William Heyen's hospitalized friend rages, averse to all experience, hating everything. Attempting to escape that ugly mood, Heyen summons the image of his "mountain ash in white bloom, // at home, where I longed to be." But in his mind the tree becomes host to "airstreams of bees" that "glide maddened / for blossoms of white filth," and his thoughts drift to pus, maggots, pond-scum—analogies that insightfully situate his friend within nature's foul and beautiful processes. The trajectory of Heyen's own thoughts anticipates his friend's insistence that life and death incite his obsessive hatred: "I hate children, I hate the dead" ("The Ash").

Expedient medical protocols can also preempt understanding, self-efficacy, and the stimulus to develop a supportive community (perhaps including a therapist) precisely when crisis smuggles opportunity into a person's life. Because he knows that "lithium would kill him," Martin, in Enid Shomer's "My Friend Who Sings Before Breakfast," makes a desperate effort at "healing / himself" (an allusion, no doubt, to the Biblical proverb, "Physician, heal thyself"). His "disease / shaped like a learning / curve" is hard to master, but compare his effort with the sad defeat of the woman in Susan Hahn's "The Shape of Happiness":

> Who she was
> has become a memory
> even for her, all chances
> for happiness given up
>
> to chemistry. Her only word was a helpless
> *yes* when the doctor suggested fistfuls
> of pills

Other poets explore familial issues. In "Arrow," Nina Nyhart ironically admits that "a gift for depression" runs through her family like "an arrow / whose sharp trajectory / none of us has escaped," a genetic concern that Belle Waring echoes in "Bipolar Affective Disorder as Possible Adaptive Advantage." Addressing a cousin, she invokes a common ancestor, "somebody with a mad talent for the trance," whose influence extends from a time when, "If you fell down raving, the tribe would attend you— / You'd wake with song-stories to make pictures in the mind." Sensing hereditary emotional patterns, family lines that perhaps transmit a predisposition to disturbance, these poets remind us that these patterns exist within an ultimately communal framework. Stories like the one Richard Krawiec tells in "God's Face" bear witness to the almost unbearable pain that pervades an entire family when a loved one is consumed by psychosis, which is a potential feature of manic-depression.

The book's sixth section looks at artists who suffered severe moods. Peter Cooley's "Irises" and "The Enclosed Field," both from *The Van Gogh Notebook*, and Linda Bierds's "Träumerei," about Robert Schumann, exquisitely envision the heightened sensual receptivity and plummeting despair we know these artists experienced. After reading Virginia Woolf's final diary entry, in which she uncompromisingly commands herself to "Observe everything," Robert J. Levy lyrically ushers her idea further: "for by doing so, / one is lifted up on a great wave / of luminous minutiae" ("Meditation on Virginia Woolf's Final Diary Entry, Written Three Weeks Before Her Suicide"). Reflecting on John Clare's wild existence, David Baker realizes, "More and more I recognize the torment / in another's mind better than my own," and, recalling his own family's "pharmaceutical catalog," sensibly comments, "It kills me to think what a decent pill / might have meant to the man" ("Bedlam"). Edwin Muir sums up the value these poems hold when he describes imagination as "that power by which we apprehend living beings and living creatures in their individuality, as they live and move, and not as ideas or categories." Contemplating Homer's ability to conceive the grief of Priam and Hecuba, Muir argues that imagination

> takes us into the feelings and thoughts of these legendary figures, and makes us feel the full weight and the uniqueness of their lives. It is as important as anything can be that we should be able to do this, for it makes us understand human life vividly and intimately in ourselves because we have felt it in others. . . . The life and movement and individuality of human beings . . . their feelings and moods and mischances, are everything to it. Compared with science its scope is vague and incommensurable, since it embraces all possibilities of experience. Consequently, it is for human living that imagination is indispensable.[24]

The last sections—"Daily Shifts" and "With the Seasons"—include poems that portray oscillating moods and demonstrate their frequently rhythmic significance. Anthony Hecht's subtle six-line poem "Retreat," with its precise verbs, succinctly expresses emotional flux. In a scene where "Day peters out" and "Darkness wells up / From wheelrut, culvert, vacant drain," his adjective "vacant" signals the hollowness of despair. Yet faith remains in a remote detail: "But still a rooster glints with life, / High on a church's weather-vane." In "The Mood Museum: *Anxiety*," Marcia Southwick worries:

> My mind is revving too fast
> like an engine smelling of diesel.
> The rain utters its keynote address,
> and tomorrow the sun will want to interview me
> in its harsh light. What should I do?

Her poem's abrupt, declarative sentences describe anxious, troubling thoughts that loom throughout the day and build up pressure that punctuates her question, "What should I do?" She repeats that appeal to end the poem, seeking a way to persevere.

Alternating moods mirror alternating seasons, so it makes sense that these poems invoke dependable seasonal metaphors. Jane Flanders refers to a moodlike "nameless season / that grips us from within." Compared to a pond stirring under ice, that internal state is, she feels, "far colder, darker, / very still" ("Stasis"). One season's mood may extend to many seasons, and the cycles of moods may even be measured in years. As Hayden Carruth fatalistically concedes in "Depression": "The cells of one's body renew themselves every / seven years—is that right? And so does one's / depression." Also physically attuned, Linda Pastan observes the internal and external signals that her body gives of atmospheric changes and acknowledges: "Some live in the storm's eye only. / I rise and fall / with the barometer, / holding on for my life" ("Hurricane Watch"). Her poem draws attention to the fact that our bodies respond to our environment in ways that can intensify emotions. C. K. Williams' "Dominion: Depression" broods on an infernal scene: locusts breeding in a field. What does this have to do with depression? Williams compares the cluster of seething locusts—"limbs, antennas, and wings all tangled together"—to neurons; the mass of them is "so dense, so hard," as indeed a mood might be. The potential for relief comes only from an abstract, disembodied "wingbeat of the innocent void moving in again over the world," as if a vast shadow or night will cool that broiling disturbance. It is a poem rich with physical imagery—language engrossed (as all these poems are) with the vivid seizure of being.

—*Thom Schramm*
Seattle, September 2007

A NOTE ON THE
COLLECTION PROCESS

Except in one case, I chose poems after corresponding with writers who responded to published calls for submissions or to a solicitation I sent to hundreds of poets selected fairly arbitrarily. In several cases, I requested a particular poem that I had read prior to contact with the poet. It would be a mistake to conclude, whether on the basis of their poetry or the fact of their inclusion in this volume, that any of these writers meets the criteria for a psychiatric diagnosis.—T.S.

A LITTLE POEM

We say that some are mad. In fact
if we have all the words and we
make madness mean the way they act
then they as all of us can see

are surely mad. And then again
if they have all the words and call
madness something else, well then—
well then, they are not mad at all.

—Miller Williams

HOW IT IS

William Matthews
Manic

I did not know, any longer,
the meaning of my happiness;
it held me unexplained.

—Eudora Welty

Out I would go, as if out were a city,
and I was buoyant and self-absorbed,
my own climate, though like a pond
my city held its own warm and chill
districts aloof to the good news and puzzle
of my self. I felt like a child with his first
library card: all bound sadness was my glee.
I thought every book was meant for me,
like a warehouse of pets, and I carried
my special, pled-for limit of six books
per visit like a scepter through the aisles.
Six empty cages. . . . At home I'd line them up
and open the first box of trances
and soon I'd have lived in each one.
I liked to walk as long as it took
to begin to spend attention outside me.
I feel like I'm talking your ear off,
when all I wanted was to describe
one of my walks, like the one that took me
at noon to The Broadway Clock Shop.
Oh I had no ambitions, like a storm,
to be anywhere specific, and then a whole
migration of brass birds left and returned
while I stood there and ignorance
ran up and down my body like a squirrel.

William Matthews
Depressive

No wonder it feels like a chore,
by the hour, the ounce, the follicle,
and no wonder we'd be more bored
without our boring jobs than we are
on the greyest Monday. It's work,
being depressed, and we're tired,
and we fall asleep and dream
and wake like the skim of fat on a broth,
and again work is before us,
in rivulet, in gram, in decibel.
And work is before us in grime,
and in erosion, and in rust.
No wonder we're too busy to rejoice,
unless work is rejoicing,
and indelible, no wonder, the story
of our lives, lumpy with anecdote.

No wonder if we fumble our explanations
of ourselves, like rosaries,
and no wonder we never lose them,
we've saved their lives so many times.
And since sleep doesn't work,
no wonder we mate with ourselves
like this, waiting to see if we
come by, and we do and we go on,
no wonder. For the work of being
depressed is to stay depressed,
the way the work of dreams is to guard
sleep by expanding the fort:
if an alarm should ring the dream
will invent an occasion for bells—
a wedding, a fire, an evening of music,
roll call at the bell foundry—
so that the bells sing out their single

notes, their names, their explanations.
No wonder we love sad songs,
or that when we remember habit
it seems to have been joy itself.
And holidays! The turkey is stuffed
with memories of turkey.
The light seems to come from what's lit,
the way it does in good paintings,
and no wonder. We'll leave our love
for the world where we can, like a dust,
like a prairie of eggs that won't hatch,
a gift too good for us to keep or leave,
and then we'll raise our glasses
just the way we did last year—
a few details are skewed: for extra
credit what's wrong with this picture?—
to its passing, and our own.

Lyn Lifshin
depression

stinks like some
smell you can't
imagine coming
from you. you
camouflage what
fills the room
with musk incense
when the wind's
wild and branches
scrape paint off
a house in one
night. you ignore
it then it comes
back like a spot
of sap in wood
that never dries
leaks thru the
enamel you burn
out of your
dreams and it
glows in ashes

Joyce Carol Oates
Mania: Early Phase

How you love everything that flies
at you!—the world's in gear, food tastes,
colors bleed beyond their boundaries
but feel right, your tongue numbs
in anticipation. While others prepare
their statements: *We saw it coming.*
We were there, we saw. All the way from
the Caribbean, the Amazon, Cape Horn—
that lethal gale.

Steven Cramer
Bipolar

Just after the downpour moves on, and it's
still a swamp of viridian and emerald
indoors and out; and the central power grid,
iffy at best, still sputters and spits;

and the citizens, alert, still hunch
by their wavering flames, tensed for the flinch
between each white shock and its thunderclap
(relaxing, a bit, as quiet widens the gap)—

it's then this German-folktale kind of calm
seeps in: brown of the briar rose, a bone-
meal wariness, the green tone of *once upon
a time, a woodman and his wife wanted children*—

and soon children came. That's the time
to pray whoever loves you escaped harm.

Jane Kenyon

Happiness

There's just no accounting for happiness,
or the way it turns up like a prodigal
who comes back to the dust at your feet
having squandered a fortune far away.

And how can you not forgive?
You make a feast in honor of what
was lost, and take from its place the finest
garment, which you saved for an occasion
you could not imagine, and you weep night and day
to know that you were not abandoned,
that happiness saved its most extreme form
for you alone.

No, happiness is the uncle you never
knew about, who flies a single-engine plane
onto the grassy landing strip, hitchhikes
into town, and inquires at every door
until he finds you asleep midafternoon
as you so often are during the unmerciful
hours of your despair.

It comes to the monk in his cell.
It comes to the woman sweeping the street
with a birch broom, to the child
whose mother has passed out from drink.
It comes to the lover, to the dog chewing
a sock, to the pusher, to the basket maker,
and to the clerk stacking cans of carrots
in the night.
            It even comes to the boulder
in the perpetual shade of pine barrens,
to rain falling on the open sea,
to the wineglass, weary of holding wine.

Michael Blumenthal
Sadness

Sooner or later it comes to everyone:
the beautiful prom queen who has lost a breast,
the Don Juan of the tenth grade who has
turned up impotent, the fleet chiropodist
who has developed a limp. Sooner or later it comes,
and you are never prepared for it quite yet,
you had hoped to be spared through yet another epoch
of your rightful happiness, you who had always
given to charity. Like a gargantuan tackle
lumbering toward you, it comes and comes,
and—though you may double lateral all you wish,
though you may throw a perfect spiral
up the middle to some ecstatic receiver
and be blissed blue-green some night
by the ministrations of strangers—it will not
spare you. It comes and comes, inevitable
as sunrise, palpable as longing,
and we must go on
laughing it right in the face
until it learns to sing again.

Susan Hahn

Mania

Sometimes I talk too much
at a shrill pitch and the bitch
part of me carries off
my conversation in directions
I'd never travel with more peaceful
lips. But when my brain swells
and pushes on the small bones
of my face, what spills out
seems so rich. I think
everyone loves me so much.
Until, alone with the bloated
moon, I hear the rattle
of my voice and its twist—
the gnarled path it takes running
after any catch, grabbing
first place in a race
it does not want to enter,
accepting the trophy
with a curtsy practiced
for royalty. Hater of both halves
of myself—raving
slave, desperate dictator.

Chana Bloch

Eclipse

There are two bodies floating above us:
                                    They are one body,
yours dark, a silence
                              tails of flame lashing the emptiness,
growing in space,
                                    emptiness opening its mouth wide
mine a ring of fire clenched around it.
                                    to swallow the fire.

Brian Swann

Circus Framework

Terror is / Such a humiliating spectacle.

—Hayden Carruth

The agony of achieving balance reproduces
     the illusion of depth, with humans
reduced to six-inch fingerlings or blown up
     to titans. So, to bolster psychic boundaries,
despite myself I find myself
     part of this lonely argument in which
nothing stays long, washed by the ebb
     and flow into an orchestration
before any briefly achieved ratios can settle
     back exhausted into the usual
circus framework. Frustrated again, I could
     settle for any familiar arrangement,
a close-up under an umbrella, say,
     full face, with thin lips, posed
as moon on the moonstruck, wintry sunshine
     of silent days . . . if it weren't for the
skidding of all objects, and the attendant
     mobile army, off into melodrama with
gags scattered like hogfeed. And the fight, the flight,
     goes on. Plans are merely distractions, a regrouping
of individuals under private warring banners
     in almost limitless numbers. Any deduction
seems logical, any relationship works
     as the truth. Hidden things become
blatant objects that glow to gesture,
     gesture gels to image. This too
I could believe in, even if divided
     among split screens with a taste
for pantomime, where, at the end, someone
     puts the houselights off, and an endless
stream of sweepers makes
     obscene use of the growing phosphorescence.

Lyn Lifshin
Depression

a dark you dream
you could curl in
shut out the cold
hanging in the
house like an
electric blanket
only you're drenched
in sweat every
thing inside's a
knife that slits
the cords short
circuits night
shocks you into
numbness leaving
just the smell of
what was burning

David Ignatow

"Holes I want to creep into"

Holes I want to creep into
and pull the cover over me
darken my mind.
I'll learn how it feels
to feel nothing.

I have a glowing heart
in an empty space.
I lie down beside it
and warm myself.

Brigit Kelly

Figure of Distress in a Field

Deep in the brain, far back.

—Roethke

Inheritance has its tools: cruel
Or otherwise:

The forsythia's nitric yellow shatters the thin air: the thin
Panes of spent denial and

Full the hurt comes down: the heart-
Down flight that shapes

Like a surgeon the being: the borne
Burden. Wet color

Shoots from the flowers: and birds like squibs fire: they rise
And fall: small birds: without color: not like

The crow: the fielded
Deceiver: fat with boss

And glossiness: his sliding
Black wings flare white in the sun: flare

One: flare two: hot
Staring steel white

And deadly to the touch. But
Compeer, too. The crow

Is accomplice: he tries
The trust: this bitterness

Of thought and its better brothers. The dark bird
Is the dead earnest of

Always here: a stone
Thrown at a target

Thrown back: and back
Into the farthest brain:

Where the bush: the fountain:
The bush burns:

In its disturbance:
In its tree.

Jane Kenyon

Having It Out with Melancholy

> *If many remedies are prescribed*
> *for an illness, you may be certain*
> *that the illness has no cure.*

> —A. P. Chekhov, *The Cherry Orchard*

I. FROM THE NURSERY

When I was born, you waited
behind a pile of linen in the nursery,
and when we were alone, you lay down
on top of me, pressing
the bile of desolation into every pore.

And from that day on
everything under the sun and moon
made me sad—even the yellow
wooden beads that slid and spun
along a spindle on my crib.

You taught me to exist without gratitude.
You ruined my manners toward God:
"We're here simply to wait for death;
the pleasures of earth are overrated."

I only appeared to belong to my mother,
to live among blocks and cotton undershirts
with snaps; among red tin lunch boxes
and report cards in ugly brown slipcases.
I was already yours—the anti-urge,
the mutilator of souls.

2. BOTTLES

Elavil, Ludiomil, Doxepin,
Norpramin, Prozac, Lithium, Xanax,
Wellbutrin, Parnate, Nardil, Zoloft.
The coated ones smell sweet or have
no smell; the powdery ones smell
like the chemistry lab at school
that made me hold my breath.

3. SUGGESTION FROM A FRIEND

You wouldn't be so depressed
if you really believed in God.

4. OFTEN

Often I go to bed as soon after dinner
as seems adult
(I mean I try to wait for dark)
in order to push away
from the massive pain in sleep's
frail wicker coracle.

5. ONCE THERE WAS A LIGHT

Once, in my early thirties, I saw
that I was a speck of light in the great
river of light that undulates through time.

I was floating with the whole
human family. We were all colors—those
who are living now, those who have died,
those who are not yet born. For a few

moments I floated, completely calm,
and I no longer hated having to exist.

Like a crow who smells hot blood
you came flying to pull me out
of the glowing stream.
"I'll hold you up. I never let my dear
ones drown!" After that, I wept for days.

6. IN AND OUT

The dog searches until he finds me
upstairs, lies down with a clatter
of elbows, puts his head on my foot.

Sometimes the sound of his breathing
saves my life—in and out, in
and out; a pause, a long sigh . . .

7. PARDON

A piece of burned meat
wears my clothes, speaks
in my voice, dispatches obligations
haltingly, or not at all.
It is tired of trying
to be stouthearted, tired
beyond measure.

We move on to the monoamine
oxidase inhibitors. Day and night
I feel as if I had drunk six cups
of coffee, but the pain stops
abruptly. With the wonder
and bitterness of someone pardoned
for a crime she did not commit
I come back to marriage and friends,

to pink, fringed hollyhocks; come back
to my desk, books, and chair.

8. CREDO

Pharmaceutical wonders are at work
but I believe only in this moment
of well-being. Unholy ghost,
you are certain to come again.

Coarse, mean, you'll put your feet
on the coffee table, lean back,
and turn me into someone who can't
take the trouble to speak; someone
who can't sleep, or who does nothing
but sleep; can't read, or call
for an appointment for help.

There is nothing I can do
against your coming.
When I awake, I am still with thee.

9. WOOD THRUSH

High on Nardil and June light
I wake at four,
waiting greedily for the first
note of the wood thrush. Easeful air
presses through the screen
with the wild, complex song
of the bird, and I am overcome

by ordinary contentment.
What hurt me so terribly
all my life until this moment?
How I love the small, swiftly
beating heart of the bird
singing in the great maples;
its bright, unequivocal eye.

IN THE MOOD

Daniel Halpern
Rock Star Dream

I'm way up there right now.
My hair rolls
beyond the wings of my back—
Hard rock I'm talking now,
electric animal pumping
the rubber housing my blood
drums sound into.
I'm in it, out of it, cool
as steel string before the juice
goes on. On stage I'm all oil,
amped-up and jagged with sound,
dreaming, the magic whip
of a drummer's stick on white skin,
the attention I give myself
fully revved in the lime-tart taste,
plugged in for those
who dream rock, rock-hearted
rubber-veined dreamers who fix me,
full of sound,
up there,
god damn yes,
up there.

Peter Klappert
This

So much for gymnastics, acrobatics, high
ropes and disdain. So much for pinnacles, penthouses,
glass rooms in the vertigo of sunlight.
Now you can hear the elevator castanets
and the dumbwaiter on its morning climb to Mme. Prudhomme
and her fishheads, now touch this caked soil
with its clutch of exhausted ferns,
these black, splintered strollers.
                    First rung or last, beginning
of ascent or cobweb's light,
house of albinos, slipped foundation,
terminus of fractures.
This last place of pilgrimage, this collapsed
chair of the mother, discarded crutch, splayed footing,
premise of stained mattress, this fulcrum
without lever, hold of all migration, sanctuary flop
cold or warm as any other. This, then. A hard place
from which to go lower.

Marcia Southwick
Interiors

Why does the interior of my room
look appalled, the chairs huddled together in silence

as if waiting for the sudden blow of an axe?

When I pull down the shade and let go,
it rolls up again, the sunlight rushing in as if to say

"Isn't there some mistake?"

I haven't thought of food for days,
and I'm dreaming about the hidden meanings of light.

■

My fear is turning itself into an endless white street.

Today the birds singing are an act of the imagination,

and night is a destination to avoid if possible
in which all of the statues come back to life.

Part of me is missing,
leaving a hole through which one can observe the sunset.

■

The empty page glares at me.
I'll drive a rusty nail into the heart of the matter.

Yesterday the sun was hurting me, burning little patches of skin
through the holes in my clothes.

Tomorrow I'll get up, wash my face, and forget all this.

As daylight breaks, dividing light from dark,
casting everything I'm dreaming into doubt,

my ancestors will turn their faces to the wall.

■

The trees go wild, thrashing in the wind. What good am I?

(I'm not an invalid, I'm just incapable of really living.
The days fly by, the sunsets flushed with rage.
If I open the door, I'm asking for it.

The walls are so strong, they could beat me up.)

It's a miracle that the fly trapped between
the window and the screen is still alive.

■

The roses are in a trance. They're trying to break free.

I'm here as if I were pinned under glass.

The grass listens without a point of view,
and the stones have waited for so many years. But for what?

The sky watches every move I make

and there are no witnesses to testify
that this is happening in my own back yard.

A flurry of anxiety turns into snow.

■

I've got my fistful of fear, and my untrustworthy sidelong glance.
I've got my narcotized smile.

I haunt someone else's life as I stumble,

a sleepwalker, my threadbare coat hugging me, my future
floating ahead of me like a nervous cloud.

Is the body the soul's clumsy partner by default?

In the Afterlife, there's nothing—

just God's gambling addiction and endless casinos of light.

The whole place rots a little, smelling of moss.

And the angels have a passion for gossip.

Robert Mezey

No Country You Remember

But for the steady wash of rain,
The house is quiet now. Outside,
An occasional car moves past the lawn
And leaves the stillness purified.

I find myself in a dark chair
Idly picking a banjo, lost
In reveries of another time,
Thinking at what heavy cost

I came to this particular place,
This house in which I let my life
Play out its subterranean plot,
My Christian and enduring wife.

What if I paid for what I got?
Nothing can so exhaust the heart
As boredom and self-loathing do,
Which are the poisons of my art.

All day I resurrect the past.
This instrument I love so ill
Hammers and rings and when I wish,
Lies in its coffin and is still.

I dream of winter mornings when
Between bare woods and a wrecked shack
I came down deep encrusted slopes,
A bag of dead birds at my back,

Then let my mind go blank and smile
For what small game the mind demands,
As dead time flickers in the blind
Articulation of my hands.

I know you must despise me, you
Who judge and measure everything
And live by little absolutes—
What would you like to hear me sing?

A strophe on the wasted life?
Some verses dealing with my fall?
Or would you care to contemplate
My contemplation of the wall?

I write from down here, where I live.
In the cold light of a dying day,
The covered page looks cold and dead.
And what more is there to say

Except, you read this in a dream.
I wrote nothing. I sat and ate
Some frozen dinner while I watched
The Late Show, and the Late Late.

Alane Rollings

The Logic of Opposites

The leaves are falling, falling as if from far up
as if orchards were dying high in space.
Each leaf falls as if it were motioning, "No."

—Rilke, "Autumn"

Serbia is on my back; Waco was my failure.
And Birmingham, Hiroshima, Belfast: I'm implicated
in the world's disgraces. Every mood is in me, every feeling.

Chain reactions blow up laboratories, cities.
When they take place in my head, they tip my balance.
Like someone plunging from a height, I fill with terror,
with "What did I do wrong?" with "Make this not be happening,"
with "Let me out of life's vicious double-crossing trick."
I fall. I beg my bones, "Get ready not to break!"
I want to play touch football in your yard again.

Let's see what links events and moods
and why I'm always drawn into catastrophe scenarios.
I miss happiness.
I want this graveyard spiral over with, the future rolling,
our clothes flying off again, and no more images
of leg-bits and exposed bones.

You don't think up and down have much in common.
You tell me one can only fall so far, can ascend to any height.
You send fragile capsules full of delicate machinery
into space, sure you'll catch them later.
I'm imagining black holes, poisoned oceans, fallout from
    precision bombs.
I'd rather have your lab coat, your van, your house,
    your crabapples,
your Hefty bag of dead grass, dandelions, dog droppings.
Mostly, I want *you* to have another piece of my mind:

To look into your eyes is a suicidal leap.
Your ideas confuse me, mix and don't mix with my own.
I can't love, can't not love you, can't not blame, can't
   blame you,
can't stand not to understand one thing
on my way down.

There has to be another mood.
If I'm tough on life, it's just that I'm attached to it.
   Though I've never asked for the heights of happiness,
I'll pray for a miraculous recovery.
   Maybe I can breathe differently, raise my head.
If my eyes weren't ashamed of the light falling into them,
I could go running with your Labradors again.

The sun has reached its nadir.
Now the days will gain upon the nights:
it's the logic of things in opposition.
   I want to fall in love with you again, lie down upon
whatever has accumulated in soft heaps beneath us:
goosedown, fallen leaves, failures, errors, and illusions.
Take my hands. Uncertain of their chances, I'm extending
   them to you.

At times, things settle into place.
I reached for the sun at noon; a tenth of a watt
lit sweetly on my fingertip.

Let's study frailty:
tiny flies in our wine; girls who slip from ramps at beauty pageants;
intellectuals forced out of Shanghai's windows;
Lebanon; South Africa; Sudan.
   Computers gently parachute to Venus. I'm on my feet,
noticing the shaft of light that's holding up the room.

Peter Cooley

Returning from the Shopping Center to the Suburbs

I drive with the brights on
like antlers to the dark. It's hard
to get ahead these days; you know,
while your soul keeps panting up behind you,
licking your collar of its salt.

Tonight again I do it: drop the wheel
& pull my eyes into a fist: I see them,
God, I swear it, I can taste the roots,
that sweet bone marrow of the stars.

I start to die, right here & get reborn
before the car I'm facing now head-on
swerves on its horn out of the road.

Cooley, you're not even high & yet
you know it: I'm among the chosen. Like
those stars I'm going to live forever, listener,
not that you asked. And while we're at it:
how do you get through your life?

Liz Rosenberg

Fighting Despair: A Haiku Sequence

Cars rush by, one sound
after another. Clear space
above fallen leaves.

I had a good lunch,
said my dad's roommate. First words
between men in wards.

Cry of the fall birds,
like gulls, the wavering calls
above waves of cold.

Contain me, that's good.
No bad dreams for the moment,
waking all the time.

Oh, God! God!—Calm down,
says my son, looking at me,
holding my big hand.

Liz Rosenberg

The Depression: Triple Haiku

My son, with infinite wisdom asks, "Tree, aren't you glad to be
  alive?"
The tree in its great wisdom, stick thin, doesn't answer, bows to
  the wind.
But I—sick with ambition, terrified, ungrateful bone-bag—am not
  glad.

David Ignatow
I'm Sure

I'm sure trees are depressed also; they are so silent except
when the wind blows, but notice how abundantly they
grow their leaves and how tall they manage to become,
thick around the waist like wrestlers. They wrestle with
the wind. I could learn from them. Their leaves rattle and
hiss among themselves as if leaves are grown to express
depression. But see how thickly they grow upon the
branch and what shade they give to persons passing or
seated beneath. It's an odd function for a depressed tree.
I was about to try a razor on my wrist.

Marcia Southwick

Born Again in a Moment of Amnesia

My heartbeat resounds in the future
of a newborn, where the air is so quiet
that trees are scared into stillness.
Then the future is snatched from me,
replaced by a sense of despair
that crushes the landscape,
knocking the trees into a coma.
And I sit here, my sorrow a stencil cut-out
through which I can see my own negative thinking
in reverse, cast out into the world,
in the form of a sagging wisteria
or the slump of a loved one's shoulders.
Should I be ashamed of this house
setting itself apart, distanced from the street
by a neatly-trimmed lawn?
Should I refuse to mirror the rain's madness
as it beats the ground, filling the sidewalk's cracks
with its disgraceful urge to wash everything clean?
Its hypnotic rhythm lobotomizes the streets.
Will those streets end in a fiasco of light
beyond the horizon of my knowledge,
where Doubt reverberates through the heavens?
It would be wrong to think that the gods
are at close range. Their language is a code
impossible to decipher, like the tapping of rain,
almost but not quite making sense,
in this arrested moment making me its heroine
for a brief time, and a brief time only,
in the charmed circle of memory.
Why can't I change my thoughts
into stars bright enough to lead the way?
I'm flying back into myself at birth,
where just now I'm beginning to cough,
shocked into existence by a hand

slapping my back, the hand of someone
who wears white and cures
the silences of those just emerging from the womb.

David Ignatow
Spinning

I hold my hands out to you
but you say your hands
do not exist. You also say
that I do not have hands,
that I have an illusion of hands
and that speaking to you
is speaking to myself,
appealing to myself
to be at one with me.
You show me what you mean
by spinning, standing
in one place—a humming top.
It delights you
and you urge me on.
I begin to turn
as I begin to weep.

Jeffrey Zable
Parallax

Every picture
turns itself around
becomes vision
in the corner of an eye.

Your hands
around my throat
are a summer breeze
oozing itself
through a window.

Gently I watch
the dark take form

cover me with kisses.

Diana Chang
A Dead Heart

It is stony,
empty as a frame of light.

I try to breathe around it
but I am its house.

In my eyes
an unmoving world.

It is close to nothing.
I am too much.

Erica Dawson
Disorder

For some diagnoses, the appropriate code depends on
further specification.

—American Psychiatric Association,
Diagnostic and Statistical Manual of Mental Disorders

I'm systematically deranged.
Two. Nine. Six. Three. I've multiplied
The digits, switched, then disarranged
The code, prognoses side by side.
And I begin. I'm certified,
Depressed, no symptoms to decode—
The signifier signified
In this recurring episode.

And then the code is rearranged—
Two. Nine. Six. O, a manic ride.
It's me, sleeping all day exchanged
For vacuuming, a quickened stride.
With spasms, ticks, I'm bona fide
Fucked up, bipolar antipode
And looking at the small divide
In this recurring episode.

But wait, the code is interchanged—
Two. Six. Three. I can step beside
Myself and leave me there, estranged.
Delirium's like suicide
Without the mess, more dignified.
Now bury me in my abode
Twelve feet under. Pretend I've died
In this recurring episode.

Yet I wake up, always inside
This room, writing the palinode—
Two. Nine. Six. Three—identified
In this recurring episode.

Patricia Vermillion
St. Dympna and St. Ottilia

They push through knot-holes
in doors I locked years ago.
Capture the Flag gate crashers,
Drop the Handkerchief screamers,
manic-depressives, all of them
King of the Mountain.
They ring around, lock wrists,
chant *Red Rover, come over, over,*
until I duck London Bridge style—
escape while they lower arms and sing
Off to prison you must go.

In my contrary garden, comfort comes
from lemon balm, meadow rue
and one great blue lobelia.
I crush garlic cloves in my left hand—
invoke the names of St. Dympna,
St. Ottilia, turn away
as Humpty-Dumpty threatens to fall again.

Delivered from those who walk
out of memories into dreams,
forced to see hair pulling, cup throwing
violence, I play quiet games
in the dark. *Button, button
who has the button?*
I refuse to say I do!

Tino Villanueva

Shaking Off the Dark

I am less constant
in this cold wind that does not rise,
that does not rest.
Thoughts fall over with sleep
I cannot command.
Shook heart of the ruined age
is what I've become.

Distraught,
mad-eyed from told formulas
bound to rule my easy ways,
I look, I see,
but fail once more to know.
Such rites of life
can waste the wit;
can be like strictures
rushing to the head.
Mine is a palpable body
that cannot stand itself.

Yet, a rebellion overtakes the mind,
the kind that breaks the shadow's hold:
I ram a fist into the howl of the wind,
shake off the dark locked
within the hell of these rare depths.
The common street
and shifting sky become a song.

I've come to rest on a conviction:
No praise for women like that
nor men
who've lost triumphant eyes,
who've quit the quick of words
with which they might have
raged forever
                for a line.

Daniel Hoffman

A Dreamer

Awakened by the clarity of dream
As the train pitched forward in a rush careening
Down the mountain—Who wouldn't scream
When the brakes fail and the conductor
Leaps from the hurtling car? It was good,
Good to clutch the reasonableness of terror,
There was reassurance in that real
Fall, real crags, a landscape of sensible
Disaster, not this nameless, numb
Dread, the humming sun a poisoned stinger.

REMEMBERING THE EPISODES

Robert Pinsky
Exile

Every few years you move
From one city to another
As if to perform this ritual.
Pictures to arrange, and furniture,

Cartons of books to shelve—
And here, bundled in newspaper,
Memory's mortal tokens, treasure
Of a life unearthed:

Clouded honey, seizures
Of hopelessness and passion,
Good nights or bad ones,
Days of minor victories and scars

Tasting of silver or iron.
Touch, loss, shouts, arts,
Gestures, whispers,
Helpless violence of sensation

Like rain flailing a window—
Then a clap of light, the body blinded
You could not say whether by
Restitution or disaster,

Clarified by tears and thunder.
Now you begin. For an instant
Everything reassures you
The long exile is over.

Suzanne Paola

Glass

In the world of the manic-depressive, there is
little that isn't self, less that isn't breakable.

—Textbook on affective disorders

You see, I became
what I saw, and kept turning—

The moon rose, and the sun rose,
and azaleas were

in gasps of lippink, and lavender, and were not.

Night fell into my mouth. Light

sometimes, and winter.
                              Summer
bloomed in my heart and there was no room! Days grew
larger, and there was no sleep.

The worm of time inside, my sickness.

Once
for a month, I didn't sleep,
watching the clock all night, the hands
skinny insects, glowing, crawling.

One secure enough to move peacefully
in its orbit, one
racing from the beak of the beating,
invisible jay.

Georgia. Thick, murderous, perfumed summer.
A woodpecker outside the window
with its steady knocking, and the oak
it begged refusing to answer—

I imagined
the career that lay ahead, film and singing,
all the people who hated me, and would try and stop me.

Eventually I cried
just answering the telephone, it seemed so beautiful,
someone lifting this instrument to hear my voice.

I'm tone-deaf,
but nothing in my life
limits me—
          I believe I could become
anything I touch.

Just that there's too much in my head,
a whole universe
stalled there, people
black-headed and laughing, a season of enormous
green, season of sticks—

Nothing can get out. So
from the body outward, I am nothing . . .

■

Do I sing?

> There is a woman who says she made me
> from her own clay and the clay of another
> under the moon's frown and the lash of oak.
> This woman who woke me out of sleep, my mother.

First, I was.

The world fell out of my eyes. It would not
return. I remember

boysized
azalea, boysized
tent of flowering quince—
                    Small world
with its own weather: no sun, pink rain.

Too much to learn. First
the turns and pathways of the skin.
The roads of the palm lead to no place of rest.

■

I set type. Small
newspaper, small town
in Virginia, full of the usual
madnesses: suicide, murder,
men who become women with a polyester swish and sheen . . .

Each story
typed in, coded by me, melody
always in my head—
                    It's exhausting
to live so much every day, to have slipped
a long-handled knife into a drunk at a blues bar,

exhausting to die like that, and still
find an abandoned newborn in a trash can,
exhausting to be that newborn,
squalling on the orange rinds and chicken bones
and newsprint violences of the discarded week.

I typed an interview
with a neurologist, a specialist
in pediatric epilepsy, almost the same,
my doctors tell me, as my disease—

I remember him saying
it's the parents are the problem, they don't want to know
their children are marred, defective, don't want them that way.

Same day, a retrospective on Krakatoa,
how its glittering
laval tongues licked the villages clean, how the gas-cloud
spewed, charring the earth's horizons

for months—

If I'm marred, I'm marred as the world is.

■

Catholic, converted
for a woman I thought I'd marry, I've given up
on religion.
Too many rules, always something
I find myself unable to believe in.

Though I loved the cardboard savor of communion, the long
wait in line for such malnourishing food—

Here three times a day
we have medication call, patients
in sweatsuits and bathrobes lined up at the nurses' station.

Where across a cosmos
of blue formica, the nurse
hands us our dixie cups of pills: lithium
with Stelazine or Thorazine, almost enough to poison . . .

After six months
of thinking, I see, doctors,
the transubstantiation you offer
in those wafers,
how they contain in their white bodies the body of the man
you want us to be—
the stable, hope-less and thought-less christ of our recovery.

And I linger at the nurses' station
waiting to line up.
Because even this most abject transformation doesn't work . . .
Not a gram of mindless peace to rebel against.

This doesn't stop me from hating you, doctors,
for your petty ambitions
for my soul.

∎

There is a woman who says she made me

I miss childhood, that parallel universe.

Fall
parading across the Blue Ridge,
                                        March snowfalls
that surprised the early, spring-
anticipating blooms.

Crocus and daffodil, flowering quince, frozen;
you'd crush the iced petals deep in your palm.

There is a woman—

When my mind turns, I hear it as the sound of glass, breaking.

Rika Lesser

On Lithium

No, I don't seem to have many side
effects: my hands imperceptibly
tremble, and it's damned hard to lose weight.
Though I appear to have more staying
power now, it's not the same. I used
to work in a tunnel, a charged field
at my desk; now the work—translating
Swedish fiction—is just a series
of tasks, queries and replies. Today
I called a German friend in D.C.,
hoping through him to find a British
chemist, all to check one word. And that
word was in English! (We did succeed.)
The *tasks* of the translator, plural,
not Benjamin's singular essay,
the daily grueling *tasks*.
                  Once I worked—
especially that summer in Finland—
ten or more hours a day. Up at
seven, breakfast prepared by a friend,
Hufvudstadsbladet, a second pot
of coffee, and I'd read books, take notes,
translate a bit—chunks of a long poem
by Enckell, read some more, write letters,
be curt on the phone if disturbed (my
friends understood), pick wildflowers,
key them out, see people now and then,
teach English to Chinese scientists,
stoke up the sauna to one hundred
Celsius . . .
              There was a shimmer
on everything. Each day shone like an
ammonite split and polished, nights like

obsidian. Even stormy days,
when I watched the layers of clouds, of
variegated grays, parade past
my windows, douse my balcony . . . No,
things are just not the same. The lightness
and speed are gone, the certainty too.
My nights and days are one. . . . Indifferent
effects of the lithium?

                    AFTER TWO

My hair is thinning, so far all in
one spot, at the nape of my neck, not
visible, thus still tolerable.
The cause may not be known. Hormonal
change is possible. But the redness
and bumps on my scalp that cortisone
won't clear point to lithium. Always
secretly vain about my hair, I
might prefer madness to baldness.
                                For
the kind I had wasn't all that bad.
Lifelong I suffered periods of
intensive work. Not always as "high"
as in Helsinki in '84
but reliably energetic.
I'd write myself into a state where
nothing but the work mattered, nothing
else existed in fact. Not heaven
exactly; still, somewhere I was calm,
oblivious of my surroundings,
of the world. A place from which all pain
was not simply shut out, but exiled.

Whither has it fled? *Wohin? Wohin?*

At present, I really can't complain.
I'm more disciplined—wake up, shower,

make coffee, work on these "crazy" poems.
But now I'm aware: of the black man
who spends his day on the steps of two
brownstones across the street, of the hum
of Astrid (my AT) or the whir
of the fan, of fire trucks, piercing scents . . .
and Music—once my constant working
companion—can't be put on, demands
all my attention. And now, too, there's
Pain, old friend, old foe, yes, Pain is here.
Events come back, flood over me as
before. What if the memories stayed
and the present vanished?

                    Just last year,
when I tried to work on these poems, I'd
fall asleep. Was I still too depressed?
The wounds too raw? Now I go on for
hours. Surely this means I've improved,
but am I better than *before*?
                Time
and again I tell myself: Why, sure;
now you are steadier, rarely have
outbursts or fits—"violent mood swings"
describes these best. Friends say I'm more
human, while I thank God the form my
illness takes is not *true* mania
I've never believed I was Jesus,
given all my possessions away,
run up astronomical charges,
awakened, rudely, in a strange place . . .
But *hypomania* was, well, it
was nice; I miss it,

                then calculate
the price I've paid in depression, of
two kinds: the lifelong malaise I've known
so well; the clinical: living hell,
two years of pain or nothing, numbness—

my Nerves like Tombs—unending Hours
of Lead (outlived)—then Chill—then Stupor—
The only letting go is getting
out, for good, or so it seems.

                                   Well then,
let's say I've come to terms, for now, out
of fear. Will another two sane years
give me the nerve to do without this
drug? I am not losing sleep, just some
dark brown and silver-gray fine hairs I'll
continue to sweep (though the parquet
is bare) secretly under the rug.

NOTES:

Hufvudstadsbladet is Helsinki's principal Swedish daily newspaper.
Astrid (AT) is a personal computer, an AST Premium 286.

Peter Meinke

The Poet to His Tongue

The day they cut my tongue out
I spit a lot of blood but
basically was pleased:
I'd nothing to say, no one heard
and the damned thing was diseased anyway:
red-white cankerroses bloomed
words burned like houses
a sentence filled a room with dead birds

I don't believe in God
but I believe
God was trying to tell me something:
shut up.

Then, I took my tongue home
not wanting to lose it (him?) completely
and curled that infected rascal up
stuffed him in a bottle of Jim Beam
(which he favored when alive)
& stuck it on the windowsill
over my desk where I nightly
in silence nod to my ex-flesh
where it spins still, turning neat
as the moon
filters through dreams & whiskey
& sometimes strange music seems
to come from it, a strain
unnatural and familiar
that speaks of love and pain
& hope & pain
& pain & pain &

but maybe it comes from the beer joint across
the street

Diana Chang

Streaming

my companion
ran alongside,
an insistent whirr

too soon too soon
slow slow
you you

she repeated loud and large

jumped into my blood
and full of temperament
beat there

be late! be late!

where to? where to? breathless, I asked,
knowing less than the shadow

urgent in my days

Reg Saner
Astrophysics

"Can't go on," sighed the heart taking leave
of its mind and throwing itself at the sun.
Ninety-three million miles in no time.

Past the mad gas of the solar corona
shot that hunk of red meat
meteoric—straight through the sun's bubble
to the wild interior, the fusion place.
Its molecules spat up their ghosts.
Its sad atoms sizzled apart like blue bees
at last incandescently happy
whizzing into and fusing with the fine-boned
nuclei of helium, iron atoms rugged as trucks,
the affluent beryllium, bedizened with neutrons.

What on earth had the heart ever wanted
beyond helping each day tell its story?

If only the brain hadn't wondered so often
why such days had ever begun.
Now their protons went freely along
with all they smacked into, knowing well
there was nothing they couldn't become,
red giant, white dwarf, down to eventual
densities smug as self-love: one pure
carbon star, many a million more times
single-minded than diamond.

"On the other hand . . ." flared the heart's
sanguine chambers . . . then retrofired
earthward in particles casual as pollen
back to the chest they had fled from.

At which the brain puzzled. "Once gone
why return? Yet why go in the first place?
As for that, why go anywhere?"

"Grown glum," said the heart, "from scrubbing
your moods, solar envy crept into me—
knowing the sun never glimpses
even one shadow. But no sooner arrived
at light's center than I learned how lost
we'd become without shadows to see by,
and how the sun kept insisting
I should still be your heart."

Alan Naslund

Granary for Pop

> *The big doors of the country barn stand open and ready,*
> *The dried grass of the harvest-time loads the slow-drawn wagon,*
> *The clear light plays on the brown and gray and green intertinged,*
> *The armfuls are pack'd to the sagging mow.*
>
> *I am there, I help, I came stretch'd atop of the load,*
> *I felt its soft jolts, one leg reclined on the other,*
> *I jump from the cross-beams and seize the clover and timothy,*
> *And roll head over heels and tangle my hair full of wisps.*

>   —Walt Whitman

Chemical conductors in the brain
quit, and the farm was far away, but
it was still a farm accident.
My head was a granary, one of those
Butler steel huts, circular, on
a circular, concrete pad, alive with
echoes, but not empty. Light stuff
in that granary, Pop: milkweed pod,
then those little two-pronged, black
weed seeds that look like angry ticks,
gorged once with blood, lots of
them, flat and black. Other seeds:
rank diseases of the land, tare,
whatever a boy could corner as his
without encroaching on his provident
father's claim: that is, all wholesome
foison of the land. And my head went
wrong, like that, an abandoned
Butler granary where a kid might
have a secret clubhouse. And there
you were, your likeness in the
clubhouse, as an ideal to be claimed
by slow emulation, Pops, a ghost.
And the other ghosts were many,

but yours flaked off the most when
my own self dried, disintegrated like
sow thistle under weed spray, 2-4D,
post-adolescent drop in brain chemicals,
perhaps, a sudden withdrawal anyway
of even the simplest rapport between
my head and how the world touched
back, returned my gaze, was there.
Strange; you may not have believed
the doctors, Pop, when they laid those
puzzling words on you, "Bipolar
Something." So just acknowledge my
country boy's mind was then as
summerfallow of worthless weeds.
Mother's harmless ghost lived
through that angry time. Yours came
a wrathful harvest, fireweed, Kochia
flaming imported, Asian colors.
Your broad, suntanned, beautiful
whole-farm-supporting, fatherly
shoulders, your polished, eye-
squinting, western face, good
as an Indian head nickel even
today—that coin lost value, too.
Salvador Dali can tell you what
you looked like when you died. I
can't. I was there, but not as
witness; my witness chemical,
gone, too. Now this is just
to say that restoration is, if of
me, then, also restoration of you.
Your dead ghost must live, to see
wild weeds bloom as true, blow as
fine as money crops, must accept
craziness, estranged for a while from
wheat, and barley, and beeves.
Yes, somehow, like Whitman, the
once solid farmer-ghost must come
in new, come in in strange joy,

rollicking from the hayfield, a
new man, not high and driving
the important load: irresponsible,
rolling like a dog in carrion,
knocking down the profitable harvest.

Dick Allen

A Lonely Stretch of Road

For months, the kind of anger that seeps
Rather than shouts through the body
Has been in me: the kind of anger
A man feels in his forties, his causes
Diminished or dull, old loves . . . old loves,
Large questions never any nearer
To being answered. It was in this
State of being that I took myself
To a lonely stretch of road at dusk,
My thoughts confused, my feelings
Unspirited as my surroundings,
Empty fields to my right and left,
Simple crossbeam telephone poles
At my side, and the thinly paved road
Unmarked except by a center line
And occasional heaves of asphalt,
Cracks and potholes. Tensed from anger,
I kept a steady pace, my eyes focused
To where the road vanished at the rise
Of a slight hill. Several large grackles
Seemed to hang in the air, behind them
The evening sun fading in a milky halation
Of sky and flabby clouds. There was little
Wind and what there was blew fitfully
At the few wild tiger lilies and irises
Growing on the banks above the crumbling
Ridges of tire tracks where a car or truck
Had unaccountably swerved. Vaguely,
I wondered how dark it would get, how long
I would have to keep on walking before I came
Out to somewhere: a crossroads,
A vegetable stand, a churchless village
In a grove of old oaks, some toothless Cunegonde
Tending her garden. But reaching
The top of a rise I found just another

Lonely stretch of road dwindling before me,
Another hill in the distance, clumps
Of withered lilacs and gnomed apple trees
A quarter mile further, I rested
On my elbows in the dusty grass
And tried to think of something
I could do with my life, some other
Way to follow. Across the fields,
A long train entered night, and there must
Have been a farmhouse hidden somewhere
Under a ridge, for a thresher was turning,
A dog was barking. The summer sky
Turned gray and deeper gray, a blur of midges
Paused a few feet over me, then swerved
To hover above the rotten and yellow-stained
Tooth of a salt block. Still, no cars,
And when I stood the road was fading quickly,
The faint scents in the air were clover,
Alfalfa, and smoke. I thought
Of all the other lonely stretches of road
I'd pushed myself across so fast
There were gaps and blurs in every year
I could remember. I let my anger
Spread to its limits and then hold steady
As I felt my way along the road by how
It was hard beneath my feet and gravelly
Or soft when I swerved off—and in that fashion
I walked until my body's simple tiredness
Forced me to stop. Faint above me, like
A voice in a long hollow tube, an airliner
Passed into nothing. I stood in the darkness,
Watching clouds drift from the stars,
Then cover them again, as if
I was to be doled out only glimpses,
Half patterns and patches of *on high*
To the end of my days. I clenched
My fingers into my palms and whispered
Angry words until the moon emerged
Like a face plunged through black curtains,

A death mask with white plaster eyes
I could not bring myself to stare into,
And cannot yet. *I cannot.* And then
It was raining and the wind picked up,
Billowing my jacket like a fat man's paunch
No sucking in of breath makes disappear.

Albert Goldbarth
Lithium Sonnet

Judith, I've seen the CPA. She showed me two
indomitable columns, numbers rising like the legs
of a statue god. And where they add up, where
they meet in a kind of pedestal at their bottom, they
declared such a sense of solidity and completion, you,
especially you, would have wept at the beauty.

And Judith, the carpenter visited. We joked about her
many minor trials, making a go of it in
a "man's world," then she got down to the monstrousness
of chainsaw, and the nearly-pubic delicacy of shavings.
At the end, she had an instrument: its bubble centers
whenever the work is centered enough to be done.

Let them be totems, let them be invoked.
For the balance. For the level.

CHARACTERS

Anthony Hecht

"And Can Ye Sing Baluloo When the Bairn Greets?"

All these years I have known of her despair.
"I was about to be happy when the abyss
Opened its mouth. It was empty, except for this
Yellowish sperm of horror that glistened there.

I tried so hard not to look as the thing grew fat
And pulsed in its bed of hair. I tried to think
Of Sister Marie Gerald, of our swaddled link
To the Lord of Hosts, the manger, and all of that.

None of it worked. And even the whip-lash wind,
To which I clung and begged to be blown away,
Didn't work. These eyes, that many have praised as gay,
Are the stale jellies of lust in which Adam sinned.

And nothing works. Sickened since God knows when,
Since early childhood when I first saw the horror,
I have spent hours alone before my mirror.
There is no cure for me in the world of men."

Susan Hahn

The Shape of Happiness

The pharmacist hands her a vial
filled with cream/green capsules
and she places them in the wide smile
of her open purse. Hopefully,
she takes them home to swallow
one by one, day by day, and prays
they'll make the world
seem brighter than the slush

she's been pushing through all March.
This winter she's seen pictures on TV
of gangsters' houses in Key Biscayne
and there are times she wants so much to live
in a walled-in, protected place,
without pain, next to dazzling water
where the evil is buried so deep
under each foundation that the beautiful women
who float above never think to see
it, their frontal lobes deadened
or so she imagines, as she accepts
the small bullet shape into her mouth
and waits for it to target
the right place in her brain.
Then, she won't care
that he's forgotten. Who she was
has become a memory
even for her, all chances
for happiness given up

to chemistry. Her only word was a helpless
yes when the doctor suggested fistfuls
of pills—pastels—that remind her of last summer's
clothes, fresh pressed, before her sweat
from the aroused sun inevitably crumpled them.

Reginald Gibbons
Question

Today? Tomorrow?
Why was he given
this happiness? Did
he ask for it in
his weakest moments?
Yes, he pleaded for
it. But did there have
to be for even
those few moments a
God who could give him
this? He hadn't thought
so but if there was
It was only strong
enough to give him
this happiness and
then leave him with no
power to keep it.
So it's going to
be taken from him,
so he'll be kicked like
a dog, crushed like a
mouse, tormented like
a bug, treated in
other words like a
human being. When?
Tomorrow? Today?

Donna Trussell
Snow

She packs her suitcase:
mad red socks
and tough denim.

He doesn't touch her.
He folds his arms,
leans against the wall.

I don't know why,
he says, people change.
He walks away.

She returns her suitcase
to the spiders
and dust. Night

brings broken sleep
and cliffs dissolving
under her shoes.

She combs her hair.
Her hands are
rubber gloves.

Four days
and she eats nothing.
Help me, she whispers.

He turns away.
She's seen that face before.
It's the face he gave

to the man downstairs
whose car was stuck
in the snow.

Alberto Alvaro Ríos

What She Had Believed All Her Life

Sometime in the night she became afraid
Of noise—loud at first, but then any
So that even the smallest motions of a cat
Unrecognized became noise, and she
Grew smaller, into the folds of the strong sheets,
Like men into the cave-like mines for copper.
As she was shrinking she became as afraid
Of disappearing as she was afraid of noise
The other way, and she wished now
    Only to stay perfectly in between,
    To live there decently
    Suspended better than any carnival trick.
But she could not balance, and whimpered
A loud sound in that moment of falling.
Together they won her this time,
Noise and pain, away and toward.
How this sound could come from inside,
Betraying what she had believed all her life,
That inside at least was a private place, hers,
    As now she heard a noise that would not stop,
    The leopards of the inside forest,
    The spiders that are darkest, all surfacing,
She could not understand, she could not.
And pain, it should not fit there.
She had taken the care to eat too much
For all the days of her tiny breathing
So that nothing more should fit.
    This surprise, this surprise,
    Like a party inside among her organs,
    But before she could fix herself up,
    Before she could plan what to wear.

Diana Chang

Mountaineering

Her house was in order in a way
when she became aware
of a labored heart
as though three chambers
hoped to do the work of four

Step after step,
balancing up there,
she inhaled thin air
like razors

Even her thoughts ached
though she framed each day
with her sight, her mind,
to record every passing sun

She had seen thousands come up,
some with the fanfare of holidays
Their heat white at those heights,
burning, she burned their light

You might say
the climb took a lot out of her

Those crumbling ledges,
the pike's clawing,
the buffeting of aspiration
and, for safety, the bite of bonds

It was mountains fed her problems,
her life honed on the axis
of their necessities

All those years she was housed
on platforms of space,
her children fastened
by the skin of her teeth,
her life in her hands
slipping

Donald Hall

from **Tubes**

I.

"Up, down, good, bad," said
the man with the tubes
up his nose, "there's lots
of variety . . .
However, notions
of balance between
extremes of fortune
are *stupid*—or at
best unobservant."
He watched as the nurse
fed pellets into
the green nozzle that
stuck from his side. "Mm,"
said the man. "Good. Yum.
(Next time more basil . . .)
When a long-desired
baby is born, what
joy! More happiness
than we find in sex,
more than we take in
success, revenge, or
wealth. But should the same
infant die, would you
measure the horror
on the same rule? Grief
weighs down the seesaw;
joy cannot budge it."

■ ■ ■

4.

"Of all illusions,"
said the man with the
tubes up his nostrils,
IVs, catheter,
and feeding nozzle,
"the silliest one
was hardest to lose.
For years I supposed
that after climbing
exhaustedly up
with pitons and ropes,
I would arrive at
last on the plateau
of walking-level
forever-among-
moss-with-red-blossoms.
But of course, of course:
A continual
climbing is the one
form of arrival
we ever come to—
unless we suppose
that the wished-for height
and house of desire
is tubes up the nose."

Angela Ball
Portrait Sketch

Woman who had never enough
never for long enough—
tenterhooks then happiness
shrilled to hysteria,
lament, dullness—

watches from a distance
rain-bleached sky, lawns'
staring green, a street
deepening with gloss—

a surface that returns incidents,
magnetic attractions, characterizations,
desires, her last heart
a midsummer pond
narrowed, glinting within leaves.

Marjorie Power
The Madwoman by Picasso

The sea is sapphire blue,
the color she lost faith in last.
The waves avoid her place in the sand
but their undertow tows her where it likes.

Neither young nor old, she stoops.
What she thinks keeps her memory asleep.
She'd forgotten her secret dancing self,
the events which left it unchaperoned.

When a man walks by,
he doesn't beckon, hiss,
or leer in her direction.
He looks away fast. She sees this.

And when, through veil or filigree
a woman glimpses her mad sister's
face, a fan flips open,
a shutter shuts.

She sees this
and the child
who stares in silence,
clutching a grown-up's hand.

FRIENDS AND FAMILY

Edward Brash

Depression

Your face—which
last week looked to me
like Ava Gardner's—
was unengaged in mental pranks that otherwise
enlighten it. Rather you were plunged by faults
across your synapses into such deep melancholy
all your eyes transported were confessions
of the pain. Your wounds were clean
examples, beautiful in their way, of
self-inflicted contests you inevitably lost: I
swear I never sensed the storm
approaching, never heard the twigs
which in the crown of wind-doomed
trees are the first to snap.

Vern Rutsala
Against Telephones

Your tears came from farther
away than long distance.
I heard them keening
from wells and mineshafts,
deep inside a darkness I know
but haven't seen. We all know
it's there, know it waits
in the closet beyond the closet
and in those canyons of ink
beneath our beds. But we don't go there.
I said, Come back. You said
you had to stay, your voice
wandering those damp caverns.
For days after that the phone
made me jump. I knew it would
be you but it never was.
I knew there was nothing I
could ever do to fish you out
whole from that dark static but I kept
waiting, waiting and jumping.

David Hernandez

from A Brief History of Antidepressants

Gwendolyn knows
them all—Wellbutrin

and Effexor, Lithium
and Celexa. Knows

the song each one
serenades to her blood.

And this is how
she scales her moods:

one to ten. One's
a head full of nightmare,

a gang of vultures
dismantling her thoughts.

Ten means she's been
kissed by rapture, means

sunlight in her veins,
a radiant heart.

Tonight, Gwendolyn
says, *I'm only a seven*,

her voice deflating
in her throat. Nowhere

near those dreadful birds
picking apart her mind.

Just three states away
from bliss, but no bus ticket

to take her there,
no truck driver to answer

her thumb's plea for a lift,
aimed toward heaven.

Enid Shomer

My Friend Who Sings Before Breakfast

Lithium would kill him,
so Martin is healing
himself: no more poetry
or fiction. When songs approach—
music and lyrics crashing down the synapses
like big boats being launched—he resists
with a journal entry: *I like the dim*
neighborhood near the prison, my
windows full of inmates,
their numbered shirts
like so many price tags . . .

He ratchets his bedtime back
an hour every twenty-four, the way you rotate
tires or crops, hoping
for symmetry even
in disrepair—Fibonacci, leaves
on a branch, this disease
shaped like a learning
curve. Still, some nights the air
will swell like a wave against his skin.
Last time he found a woman and gave her
all he owned—car, furniture,
every single book. Yesterday

he remembered what his father said
when he first saw him manic,
so incandescent with happiness
he seemed to disappear into it,
like the hottest part of a flame
that burns invisibly just above
the jet. Not "enjoy it while you can,
my boy," but "sing before breakfast,
cry before night."

Imagine a vise,
Martin says, in which you are both
the thing being held

and what holds it in place, metal
grinding on metal, that shining embrace.

William Heyen
The Ash

"Every minute, every day,
I hate this life.
I hate the trees, I hate the sunsets,
I hate my wife."

A nurse entered the room,
handed my friend his medicine,
a cup of water and two pills,
lithium and Thorazine.

Eyes glazed, sedated,
but fists clenched above his sheets:
"I hate the doctors, the meals,
the beds, the stupid illiterates

who work here." I nodded,
but tried to save myself, ignored him,
closed my eyes, thought (for this was May)
of my mountain ash in white bloom,

at home, where I longed to be,
within its perfume-menstrual smell,
pure love mixed with death
mixed with pure swill

mixed with its own being
where, toward our earth's distillate,
airstreams of bees glide maddened
for blossoms of white filth,

thought of hands dipped
into cavities of ambergris,
of tongues licking scented necks,
lips sucking pus, maggots

humming their hymn of blue flame
in a dead animal's lung,
of the rainbow glaze of mucus,
the milky beauty of pond-scum,

of my own oval of flowering ash
in evening air, those powers that sustain
my body's sick-room odors,
the twisted smiles, the sunlit skin

cancers, the hate-vapors drifting
toward my broken friend, who cried
"I hate books, I hate the seasons,
I hate children, I hate the dead."

Where, if ever, will this end?
My friend moves from one ward to another,
embedded, circling lower. For now, outside,
I circle closer to the white ash flower.

Gwen Head

Somnia

Less and less stately, in chambered disarray,
your soul shrinks to sleep. Your chevroned quilt's at war
with the zebra light of noon behind closed blinds.
For twenty years I've known that swag of hair,
those eyelashes, that hand of glazed white porcelain.
As a small child I coveted such a hand,
forget-me-nots and ribbons in its palm,

where grown-up ladies stubbed their lipsticked butts.
Your shuddering's almost stopped. Marine, becalmed,
you drift on a Sargasso Sea of Navane.
Your bad dreams stay. Life's horrors, left behind,
make nightmare sweeter than the light of day.
No one can see the knives, the blood, the rats.
No one but me can guess your laddered scars.

David Ignatow

Figures of the Human

My love, pills in her purse,
runs, now staggering, now flushed,
her speech racing near the world:
whisper talk to it, dangling,
"Let creatures ride her, soften hard bumps
for them." Who warns her from self,
racing, singing, lightfooted?
Birds, dogs, cats screech, bark, mew,
conversant with air.
                    Raise her from swooning,
the childhood spirit. Catch her
skittering, mewing with joy, barking delirium.
Then are we loved, hand drawing swiftly
figures of the human struggling awake.

Reginald Gibbons
Analytical Episodes

First, how I loved
your life of feeling—unstinting
replenishings
for my miniature heart, that grew

But everything
hurts; our own wounded consciences
won't let us be—
we hear cries next door, and we cry

In daydreams, what
I see and want—the still aura
of if only
good things could stay so forever
(Old clothes on a hook, an open summer window)

Good news chastens;
I try not to hope—what happens
blows like pale straw
in the arriving winds, past us
(I will hold the moment's happiness)

Bad news shatters;
your soul is like a lovely vase
beautiful whole
dangerous and sharp in fragments
(I will gather them for you in my hands)

Richard Krawiec

God's Face

This morning the sky is a gray fur
so close and dense the skin
of heaven remains unseen;
the blurred circle of the moon,
barely luminous, resides behind
like the empty socket
of a removed eye.

As I lift the damp newspaper,
the sharp stones of my driveway
press through my slippers.
I scan today's headline tragedy—
some figure skater was bruised
on the knee by her rival. I am too
worn out for disgust, though I drop
the paper into the thin, black stream
which flows down the gutter.

The tortured souls I love
wait anxiously for me at the window.
I turn towards them to see
three faces pressed to the glass,
three sets of dim sockets, no
visible eyes. Their need is like granite
weighting my shoulders, their silence
desperate pleas which pull me back
to the jaundiced interior
of our leaky-roofed house.
How can I save them?

My oldest son destroys
his demons in preschool fights
and tantrums thrown when recalcitrant
toys taunt him by not bending
to his will. He pounds his own head

to punish himself for his mother's illness,
punches his friends so he will not
have to punch her. His face is so torn
by anguish I fear it will scar
him worse than any knife wound.
His only escape comes through an infusion
from the pacifying tube
of the television set
where he learns there is evil
he must fight, though he's frustrated
to find the enemy in his life
has no face.

My youngest, on the verge
of language, still screams
uncontrollably each time he is touched
by this unknown woman, his mother, my
wife. Perhaps he knows
the secret she revealed to me
two hours past midnight—
that she is the one
who will murder him.
She has seen him in the crib,
seen her hand reaching,
seen his head cracked
with the splintered delicacy
of a crushed eggshell.
He spends his days stuck
to my chest like velcro,
his hands hooked into my shoulders;
a small, solid presence around
which I scramble eggs, talk
on the phone, shower and shave.

And my wife, my wife, that assortment
of nervous tics, evasive eyes, psychotic
blips and accusations, that shuffle-
gaited collection of human fragments

held together only by the loose bag
of her skin—*I've lost my self*
there is nothing there beneath
the medicine . . .

O You Lord, whose face I imagine
in this terminal sky, feral and blind
to human possibility, do You wonder
why my belief is based on doubt
of my own ability to persevere?
Is it Your judgment or Your faith
which reveals to me Your contented
blindness? Or am I mistaken,
misguided like Job, do I confuse
the cross for the cave, hell
for heaven, perseverance
for repentance?

Pamela Uschuk
To Play by Heart

for my mother

I

You do not smile
as you sit behind Father
in the picture I pinned above my desk.
A blue glass vase your mother bequeathed you
holds Sweet Williams, hiding your hands.

    The photo doesn't betray
     your lithium shake, the laughter
     that breaks on your lips.

Mother, I remember your hands
playing piano, Mozart
or Liszt, Rachmaninoff's dark
straining chords. How intelligent
they found the keys.
I loved their music, often pretending
I could play by heart as well as you.

II

What ceremony cures grief?
The Christmas your father crashed
into a semi, a few weeks after
your favorite brother suffocated,
chicken pox lining his lungs, you stabbed
out *La Polonaise* on the organ,
to make their ghosts forgive.

Makeup scribbled on your white white face,
you spun in the swivel-rocker.

Laughing, your mouth was a split tomato
of thick lipstick, your eyes
bruised inside penciled rings.

Nightly we hid from
the wound of your howls.
Neighbors kept their children
away. Your wild hands
agreed with every accusation spread.

After you stitched closed
the top and bottom of a skirt,
insisting it fit, they committed you.
Oh, Mama, the silence
was blue as your electric face.
Thorazine made you sleep, even
with your eyes open.

I held your bottle of red and grey pills
and would have taken them all for you
but I feared the way
you sliced faces from pictures
in the family album.

I learned to play French horn,
dissolving my bedroom with high E.
Watching my face bend
inside its silver bell, I gave
each note like a prayer to you
who could not listen.

III

For years now the only talk
between us is small talk, weather,
how many bread and butter pickles you put by.
You no longer play piano and I gave up

French horn before I left home.
You never ask why I have no children,
as if that was settled long ago.

In the mail, you send fall
leaves, their brittle carmine unbroken.
A miracle. I hold them
while I listen to Liszt
played like swallows
taking light in their beaks.
Night defines the desert around me.
These leaves are perfect, telling
more than any words you write.

Mother, your face waltzes, mirrored
above the keys, and I begin
to see beyond discords I've blamed you for.

> *In photos of you at my early marriage,*
> *you stare, a deaf decoupage, into*
> *buried crevasses that undermine*
> *the flat Michigan plain.*
> *Perhaps this was the register I failed*
> *to read, what you couldn't tell me*
> *of domesticity. I didn't know*
> *how I could hug you home.*

What reply can I send you now?
Mama, I learned to play
without technique
music's riddled heart.

Cheryl Savageau
Thorns

You jump in religious ecstasy
on Mémère's bed
and I jump beside you
staring at the twin hearts
floating against the blue sky
one circled by thorns
the other by roses

They're bleeding
you screech in my ear
in mid-jump
I am watching you
not the hearts
I sleep under every night
No they're not, I say
Yes, look, they're bleeding, you insist
your face flushed and sweaty
eyes wide, arms rising and falling
as you jump and stare
I struggle to see what you see
and almost I see them shimmer against
the sky, the red drops glistening

Now when I see your mother
at family weddings
I ask her about you,
how you're doing
Not so good she tells me
the doctors say
she's one of those
depressed maniacs

It's your mother who had fallen
under the hands of the priests
slain in the spirit

she lay on the wooden floor,
surrounded by shadows ululating
like babies hypnotized by their own voices

I remember you told me
how you walked the freeway in California
to get milk for your baby
no store for five miles, no car,
your husband out on a binge
how you agonized
whether to take the baby with you
finally left him in his crib
and came home to find a house
full of men—your husband
and his friends who all wanted food
and a friendly fuck
I don't remember how you escaped
their groping hands and leering
alcohol mouths, or if you did
I blot it out
but I remember how your brother
threw you down a flight of stairs,
angry that you tried to leave
his drinking buddy,
the man who beat you
You worried aloud for the next four months
that the baby you carried would be an idiot
damaged irreversibly

Gloria, you always were a maniac,
dyeing your hair green in seventh grade
for St. Patrick's day
We're not even Irish
I told you, watching in disbelief
fascinated by your daring

You pushed needles through my ears
barely numbed with ice cubes

the only time I was brave enough
to follow your lead with no holding back,
and you caught me as I fainted,
spilling rubbing alcohol across the table and floor,
my little sister running outside to tattle
to returning parents
We laughed all night under blankets

Now I hear of you through family gossip
the lost jobs, suicide attempts, hospitalizations,
the latest man doing you wrong, the saintliness
of your mother taking you in

You told me the heart with roses is Mary
the one with thorns, Christ
but I know they are both you, Gloria,
depressed maniac, adventurer,
a heart where roses bloomed
surrounded by thorns

Mémère: Pronounced *Mem'ay*; French-Canadian for "Gramma."

Nina Nyhart
Arrow

There's an axis that runs through
my father and me and my son—

no—an arrow
whose sharp trajectory
none of us has escaped

This isn't target practice
it's the real thing—

the long face, slope of the nose
freckled skin and
in the marrow bone
a gift for depression

It might have been a bullet
that traveled through us

but we're lucky
to live in primitive times
At the end: feathers

Belle Waring

Bipolar Affective Disorder as Possible Adaptive Advantage

You should have seen those mountains, cousin.
Tidal waves of frozen rock like huge implacable parents.

I buried a poem at the base of a tree. I wanted nothing—
no food no drink—just to write one thing on top of another.
I just wanted not to be scared of old Mr. Madness
   skulldugging around
sporting his diamond stubble
and on my way home, there he was—
standing in the train between two cars
on the floor plates shifting in a racket ever faster
as the train blasted into another country altogether.

I see it, cousin.
You and I had a common ancestor, time out of mind,
somebody with a mad talent for the trance,
for collapsing onto the rusty ground, for tasting the old
blood of the earth.

If you fell down raving, the tribe would attend you—
you'd wake with song-stories to make pictures in the mind.

Without those gifts, the manic-depressed
would have been just a fractious pain in the ass
and get pitched off a cliff.

The tribe would survive and they'd get to keep the art—
a thousand notes to call the ancestors back to the root.

At the onset of mania, Robert Lowell told his wife,
I can feel it in the spine. It's a funny creeping feeling . . .
coming up the spine from the lower back up.

Cousin, there's no romance in this.
So this is it. We're obligated now to survive

whether or not we still hear the green music we heard as
    babies
when Nanny held us fast so we'd calm down
and watch the window change to night.

The night was birds changing to wind.
The night all along was feeding us.

The night was a hum and a pulse in her chest
and the hurt escaping her marrow bones
from the hollow the madness had left.

Steven Cramer
Thanksgiving

Light ripens across my father's woods,
across my window's backyard view.

"Your mother and I have fixed
your old room up for you," he says—

cardtable desk, ashtray, pen,
so I can memorize again

portions of autumn sun the trees
shine back, lapidary, cold.

And I can hear the eddies of talk
lap against the wall, carrying

back those late-night monologues
from the living room, swells

of applause, brash commercials
keeping me awake past one,

when my father, manic, couldn't sleep
for weeks. Now he's calling me

to point out a purple finch
chipping from the paddock edged

by the row of adolescent pines . . .
but no, that's not quite right:

this year they're tall enough to hide
the neighbor's yard. My father waited

their lifetime for privacy.
"The back forty," he would call

his acre of sunlit birchbark
curling, shedding another year.

We sweep out the garage. He bends,
cursing, to flick a leaf-stem

from the hood of his El Dorado,
spreads out on the gravel driveway

two rakes, two brooms, pruning shears.
"Great minds think alike, and so

do fools," he says, strangely. Then:
"I'll get this place fixed up before I die."

Carole Ann Borges
Learning to Feed Ourselves

Momma had spells—what
else could you call them?
Seven days spent crying in bed,
enough water to drown a small child.

Kiss your Momma, Poppa would command,
and I'd comply, kissing like it was a last goodbye.

Funny thing was—
a week later, she'd be up and at 'em,
waving her onion-smelling hands in the air,
laughing as if nothing had happened.

After a while, it seemed natural;
I'd come home from school—
she'd have that look in her eye.

I'd open a can of kidney beans and start a salad.
Poppa would snap some Saltines in a glass.
He'd pour hot milk over the crackers.
Then, we'd just wait it out.

THE ARTIST

Paul Mariani

Mountain View with Figures

As if Cézanne had rendered it: a palimpsest
of planes, a dreamscape realized, an imbrication,
the easel facing the brilliant south exposure.

In the middle foreground a patch of vale, shadowed
by a swirl of crosshatched pines. He counts again
the colors: a tan, a green, a gray, a tan, a tan.

Beyond the graygreen strokes he feels the Absolute
malignly beckon in the bald & treeless peaks.
He stares now as he contemplates his labors,

the hesitations hissing up ahead. It is
what has kept him sleepless night after night:
fear at the edge of the abyss, empty speculations

deep enough for even an Empedocles. He knows
the most he has to paint with is a round
of absinthe sounds & acrobatic stanzas. Those

and a syntax even the boys at the Sorbonne
could nod assent to. He wants the words to paint
his naked canvas, words to ring in the Absolute

at last. He wants to feel the mountain ring.
Fool that he is, he needs to feel that, if he
climbed it now, he would find himself transfigured.

Leonard Nathan

The Poet's House Preserved as a Museum

Here by the fire, in his favorite chair,
he waited the coming of the Age of Spirit
with his friend, the philosopher, as his wife
stitched by the oil lamp on the oak table
and rain fell harder in the spring dusk
that darkened the wide window looking west.

He could, from this vantage, see far out
over the lake where the sun blazed through clouds
in a stupendous arrival of light just
before it set behind the head of his friend,
who was once more confessing the sin of doubt,
his huge brow bent helpless under shame.

The poet explained once more how all the signs
promised the Great Coming, but this time
his voice had in it something that made his wife
look up from her needle—It was the rain, she thought,
and the waiting and him so easily cast down,
but these were good times and there was tea.

Meanwhile, as summer swelled, the revolution
across the water became a bloody angel,
and one day his dearest sister stiffened
into wild silence, and then, also,
his friend, the philosopher, began drinking too much,
showing up in tears, his clothes filthy.

But visitors found the poet happy to tell them
the newer truth: that each must release the Spirit
within, though his wife could see that when he looked
beyond them west, he looked at nothing special,
and she could feel the pain of his favorite chair
as he sat himself deeper and deeper in it.

Jane Kenyon

In the Grove: The Poet at Ten

She lay on her back in the timothy
and gazed past the doddering
auburn heads of sumac.

A cloud—huge, calm,
and dignified—covered the sun
but did not, could not, put it out.

The light surged back again.

Nothing could rouse her then
from that joy so violent
it was hard to distinguish from pain.

Tino Villanueva

Now, As We Drop: A Poem of Guilt

for Anne Sexton, 1928–1974

It was for therapy you sang
from the wounded house.
It had come to that:
releasing passion from the fist;
working both ends of the clock
to death.
And those tangled images
kept coming in volumes
slim and loud.
How each poem became a resting place
on one's private journey;
how each time your breath kissed us awake.
And for awhile you
straightened out the image,

sharing it like homemade bread;
like balloons ten for a quarter.
Then the tension broke;
the cords snapped,
so you summoned what made you feel
more alive: you summoned Death,
and finally you broke into the clear,
rowing into the current waters
toward the tall-drawn
horizon framed weak for a steeple;
rowing, rowing always against the dark,
for nothing must have been lit
in the sacred height.
And there you were, engulfed in the Fall,

confessedly wrecked and undone by the fumes
of the hurried act: you against Death

Death against you
you against you
hearing Death grinding his engine,
feeling Death climbing up
your limp breath;
Death, O tasteless Death, coming
with his pale-blue eyes.
And choosing to live no more for a line
you braved it all the way,
preferring heresy to pain,
living up to your final word, that sullen act:
and *that* is no sin before any God.

But we are the Death-dealers: we who once
read your life and bought your image.
Now, as we drop
toward our sound dreams,
we toss with guilt,
and turn tangled in our sheets
as your profile cuts our sleep.

Gregory Luce

"The animal night sweats of the spirits burn"

Robert Lowell

Adrift among damp sheets you turn
and turn the pillow over seeking
the cool side that isn't there. You turn
your face to the window. Rain smears
the glass and beads the streetlamp's light.
Tires hiss along the pavement.
You turn away.
               Driftnets of feeling
wash over you in the dark
and finally carry you down to sleep, to dream
in fragments half-remembered when
the sun pours in across your face.
                    Arising
you wake to the perpetual
daily crucifixion: pinned by desire
to desire, you wriggle like an insect.

Robert J. Levy

Meditation on Virginia Woolf's Final Diary Entry, Written Three Weeks Before Her Suicide

Her last warning to herself, courtesy
of Henry James: *Observe everything.*

Observe the oncoming of age. Observe
greed. Observe my own despondency.
By that means it becomes serviceable.

Not by seeing too much do we discover
the desolation implicit in life,
but through myopic impoverishment,
a tunnel vision of the soul.
                              Sometimes
the necessary pressure of word on word
supports one for weeks at a time, and then
vanishes.
            I intend no introspection
(she notes, introspectively).
                              And, who knows,
perhaps she's already imagining
the sea applauding her late return—
by ankle, waist and brow—to undertow
and understanding.
                      Acclaim is buoyancy;
anonymity's the anchor that moors
us to our own worst selves.
                              I insist
upon spending this time to my best
advantage, she writes. *I will go down*
with my colors flying. This I see
verges on introspection;
but doesn't quite fall in.
                      It is never
the world that deserts the writer,
but the words, which sometimes evaporate

with little sighs beneath ungentle hands.
(What is despair but a loss of language
for the radiant specifics?)

Occupation is essential. And now
with some pleasure I find it's seven;
and must cook dinner. Haddock and sausage . . .

The multiplicities flood back.
                              One thinks
how language has fashioned us from dust
to eulogize the dust, to find the large
in the small, and the small in the large,
and how each dinner is sacral, unique:
this one, particularly mottled sausage
(plumply pink, waiting to explode its case)
and this individual fish (blue-gray,
cold as the ocean where it swam and died).

Observe everything, for by doing so
one is lifted up on a great wave
of luminous minutiae, spirited
both back into the world and to one's self,
toward home.
                    I think it is true that one gains
a certain hold on sausage and haddock
by writing them down.

Peter Cooley
Irises

Without your asking, certain prayers will open for you
in the morning light. They intend to be profuse.
So, like the hush folded into these green wings
huddling the faces of the irises
which exchange their radiance with each other,
the answers will be countless, wordless,
as your appeals last night.
                              Can it be,
you ask, your solace while you stare
is no more than this choir of clear, blue fire
the heat has risen from so that angels can break forth
in jubilant cold flame?
                              In the asylum at St. Rémy
Vincent put down these flowers to stem the flood,
to keep the demons from himself while he kept watch.
And as he painted the waters parted that he walk,
that he believed he walked. While he burned there he believed.

C.B. Follett
Man on Fire

for Vincent

Surely, manic is there.
Swirling stars, twisted cypress,
and the crows, flocking,
in that last day of scalded fields.

But where is *depressive* in the lush warmth
of farm bridges, peasants with sturdy limbs,
and hay wains painted from his embrace.
And the searing wheat,
hot, hot in midday's blaze.

Did he drink absinthe,
glass after tiny glass,
knocking it back for the strike
of lightning set off in his brain?
Did it shift him, short circuit
the joy and drive him
to those moments in the sun?

Chronic hunger, and oils
squeezed low. Paint, paint,
slash it on 'til the palette
blurs and the tubes are split
and spent. More paint, Theo,
send more paint. I am driven
by its smell and my own hot blood.

Unshackle a little of the madness
of passion, to do battle
with a canvas that will live
through time, setting off
an answering blaze in each viewing
after his.

Peter Cooley
The Enclosed Field

So, this, too, is a happiness, whispers the man.
He has stepped into the field, the field is his,
cut off from the horizon by a wall
unscalable, cold purple. There an olive tree
squats atop the mountain, sentry to no one.
There the houses he will never enter
nestle the foothills in chill lavender.
The sun warms nothing, it is very ill
and cannot distinguish the morning from itself.
But in the field his body is all dancing;
he is a reed, a blue anemone,
his breath reddening each poppy, each breath slumberous,
never sleeping; he is the grass
parting to take the wind into its shaking
and bend it, break it, into song. He is this song
warbled to no one, chanted along the ground
where he will lie down, no one later on
but Vincent himself, Vincent among the fumes.
He will lie down with his demons in their flowering.

Edward Hirsch

Christopher Smart

> *For they work me with their harping irons,*
> *which is a barbarous instrument, because*
> *I am more unguarded than others.*

I am the wild ass galloping through the streets
Trailing the dog star, the mad gull. I am
A white raven spilling light through the skies
Like a colorful beacon, trailing the wild ass,
The laden bull. I am the hooves and the wings

Of the mule clattering through the streets
On a wild journey to Bedlam, a journey
Into a desert of pocked houses and
A whirlpool of dead trees, dead cactus. There
Are buzzards shuddering in the vacant branches.
There is a holy ram swallowing its tongue
At the mirage of a water hole. There is
A calf inside the ram inside the bull
Swallowing its own blood. And I am kneeling

Under the calf's small belly in the street.
It's snowing. The moon is taking off her garments
Like an unruly queen; the desert prophet
Has swallowed his tongue. There are
Lizards crawling through the snow in the
Footprints of the goose, the wild ram.
The bull is weeping. And mother,

I am naked now; I am wondrous nude.
And it is still snowing. I am underneath
The knife constantly, chained at the ankles,
Squirming in my slaughtered ram's body. I am
Racing through the pocked streets under the
Moon's wild eye. The winds are howling.
The clouds are peeling away like the skin
Of a dead man's body. I am fleeing

Into the desert on a wild ass
Trailing a dog star. And believe me,
The ass is dead. Its body is hardening
Between my wild legs hardening in the cold.
The buzzards are riding out into the blizzard
To move the blood, and to moor the corpse. Because
The night is fierce; the desert winds are
Scraping along the ground. The moon is flecked
With the blood of hooves. And it's snowing.
It is always snowing in the country of the mad.

Gerald Barrax

from **Epigraphs**

2.

> *Much madness is divinest Sense—*
> *To a discerning Eye—*
>
> —Emily Dickinson

I envy you, Mr. Blake,
set screaming at four
when God looked in through your window,
and never a moment's doubt.
I believe in belief
that drives one mad,
when the darkroom door
swings open onto a nova that burns all the images
to blank white   freeze dried naked   and you hear
the uniform hiss of background noise in space
roaring in your mouth—profound terror
after the fact
and not the prudent wager,
not ashamed to say
Yes that looks like God out there to me
yes there are angels in that tree
yes I see the ghost of that flea.
If you are mad, Mr. Blake,
it's not the poet in you: the sanest of men:
what God sends poets with rifles and missions
to the tops of towers, to shopping centers, holy wars?
What poets go?
Heaven isn't that far away.
    At fifty-four I can still scream, Mr. Blake,
though I've already seen in the eye of a Humpback whale
the doomed tolerance of your face at the window.
But I'm nearly as willing to let my mind go a little,
to lean against the sun,
for one more poem.

David Baker
Bedlam

Mr. Clare has decided to walk home,
bluecaps under foot, maiden-loam, the green
abounding countryside in a sudden song.
Four years with Dr. Allen and he's been
a vapour tossed into a nothingness
of noise, Fair Mead House and Leopard's Hill Lodge,
the Northampton General Lunatic

Asylum—such awful din to the rustic
poet shuffled among them. Still, his "mental
alienation" adds potent fire
to his idylls, so Allen, whom Clare
in a snit once dubbed Dr. Bottle-Imp,
arranges patronage. July 1841.
Furze, ling and brake all mingling free and grass

forever green. He's looking for it now,
a home in the green world, yet sees hardly
a thing he knows for his own. Overhead
two birds whisk, tight-yellow-wing-tipped warblers,
lighting on a bare yew or plane tree limb.
The Gipseys are gone—one left her hat—so
he stuffs it in his pocket for *another*

opportunitty. Two days later he's
forty miles closer, running parallel
to the Great York Road, passing Labour-
in-Vain public house, then Potton, and a full
view of Bugden. He beds in a gighouse,
trussed down in clover, dreaming of Mary.
Somebody took her away from my side.

It's a buggy day in Ohio, smeared
with humid clouds. I've been hacking back brush,

lopping trees, whizzing my loud weed-eater
down fenceworks and pond's edge to curb the growth.
More and more I recognize the torment
in another's mind better than my own.
I've got a mean streak a mile wide. But why?
I've got a mouthful of weed seeds and bark
and blisters like green grapes in my hands—
gasoline sears the grass-slits up my arms.
But it's nothing a little balm won't soothe,
nothing another pill won't ease. I think
the work does me good, trimming things down
to their marrow-most clarity. When Clare
says he's *feeling very melancholly*,
he means he's been cooped up, half-crazy or
worse for years. He's in love with two women,
Patty and Mary, one real wife and one
beloved in his imaginings—
he misses his children, legitimate
and more. He wants his old life back again
at Helpston on the acres where he wrote,
of beans in blossom, luscious comes their scent.
It makes me less grim to sweat through my shirt
and rip another path among brambles.
It makes me less mean to see Ann happy
now, working inside the picket garden—
she knows the ways of every flowering,

fruit-bearing, food-making thing in the beds
she's raised a foot above the earth. That's where
she wants to be, enclosed and more at ease
by miles than if she were loose in the world
where cracked doors keep her sleepless, where roving
men mean horror and harm. I wish I could
snap my fingers and make it all better.

We're lucky to live at least as latter-
day progeny of medical progress.
Our family's pharmaceutical

catalog: Adderal, Prozac, Paxil,
Dezyrel, Wellbutrin, and the whole pink
genera of antibiotic blooms
that have kept us alive through shock, sepsis,

contagion, the tiniest of toothaches,
the cruelest of terrors. I know our meds
like the life list Clare keeps in his journals.
Got some branches of the spindle tree with
its pink colord berrys that shine beautifully
in the pale sun—found for the first time 'the
herb true love' or 'one berry' in Oxey Wood

brought a root home to set in my garden.
It kills me to think what a decent pill
might have meant to the man. He's ten miles
from home now and hasn't eaten for days.
He's hearing poems in his head, whole poems
at a time, of the thirty-five hundred
he will sing in his lifetime. He thinks he's

Child Harold in this one—sexy, heroic.
In one he grieves he's lost Love home and Mary.
He rips a tuft of grass by the roadside
and writes later it tastes something like bread.
I ate heartily till I was satisfied
and in fact the meal seemed to do me good.
In a life-sketch from Northampton, fellow
patient ("inmate," Clare huffs) G. D. Berry
draws the aged poet sunk in torpor.
He's furrowed, worn, his enlarged cranium
characteristic of long lunacy,
as Allen has it. Even his death mask
will look like a bud about to split open,
eerie smile crackling along the jaw.
In all he'll spend twenty-three years more
in asylum after these runaway days
seeking home—twenty-three years *feeble, lost,*

yet gardening the grounds on hand and knee
and writing poems and letters to ghosts.
Dear Sir I am in a Madhouse I quite
forget your Name or who you are You must
excuse Me for I have nothing To
communicate or tell Of and why I
am shut up I don't know I have Nothing
to say so I conclude Yours respectfully
—he signs it in his finest hand—*John Clare.*
He's almost here. Voices down a gravel walk.
He rests his broken feet on a heap of stone.

What he calls Bedlam Cowslip is lungwort
in our world. I've just splattered the whole batch
beside our fence with my weed-eater, gnats
and dust aspew. If she weren't laughing so
hard, Ann would kill me. But it's nothing
some replanting won't fix. She knows my back's
burning—my head full of whining and rue.

When she calls me to come look, I see
she's unearthed another nest of rabbits.
We could prog them on their way, as Clare writes
in his sonnet on mice, or let them stay
under red flaps of cabbage awhile where
they've feathered the dirt with fur. There's a strong
smell of apples and sweat in the air, scorch

of small engines, the answering yammer
of developers' saws tearing the woods
beyond our green hill. He sees chimney smoke
over the neighbors', a peat-roof. He sees
familiar petals and blades in his yard.
Yet no one's home at his home. He can walk
no more, but wanders the place *nearly hopeless.*

It kills me to think what he knows. He's come
eighty miles in four days, after four lost

years, to find them all gone. O lunatic world.
O lunatic, swelling, flowering world.
He bends to scuff some dirt around her Head-aches—
homeless and home   and half gratified
to feel that I can be happy any where

Linda Bierds

Träumerei

> *All I have done in music seems a dream*
> *I can almost imagine to have been real.*

> —Robert Schumann, 1810–1856

Perhaps this, then: the holystone licks
of the winter Rhine. A cleansing.
A scouring away. Anything to free him
from the constant filling.

Weeping, in slippers and dark robe, maddened
by phantom voices, music,
he walks from his house with
the tentative half-steps of a pheasant.
A little rain collects on his robe hem,
and street meal, the cubiform dust-chips
of cobblestones. He has carried no coin purse
and offers to the bridge guard
a silk face cloth, then the image
of a man in bedclothes, in the quarter-arc of flight

from a railing to river.
There is wind—upward—
and the parallel slaps of his slippers.
With the abrupt closure of a trumpet mute
his heart stops. Then the music, voices. Water
has flushed through his robe sleeves, and
the thin, peppered trenches
between groin and thigh.

He will surface
as an opal surfaces: one
round-shouldered curve of brocade in the wave-chop.
Then his heart kicking back.
And the oarlocks of rowers who are

dipping to save him?
A-notes and A-notes—perfect—in unison.

What else but to starve?
The starched coats of asylum guards
give a fife's chirrups. They are joined by
tintinnabulum, chorus and oboe
on his brief walks to the ice baths.

At the first flat shocks and frigid clearings
he smiles, murmurs
that his madness is at least his love,
distorted, of course, pervasive, but still . . .
aural. A music. The trees

by the fenceline fill, release. One year,
two. He follows halfway, taking
into the self the quarter-notes of
footsteps, the cacophony of laughter, wagons, doors,
the hums of the candle-snuff.
Writing stops, then speech. No word,
no flagged dot on its spidery stave
to diminish the filling. What else but

to turn from all food, to decrease from without
like the August peaches? To take at the last
the fine, unwavering balance
of an arc—heart and perimeter—
a cup where all sound resonates? . . .

A bell has fallen in Moscow, he once wrote,
so huge it carried its belfry to the ground.
And into the ground. The bell lip
and shoulder boring deep in the earth. Then
a cross-rip of belfry. Then, through
the stark reversal of summer grasses,
four pale steps leading down.

DAILY SHIFTS

Anthony Hecht

Retreat

Day peters out. Darkness wells up
  From wheelrut, culvert, vacant drain;
But still a rooster glints with life,
  High on a church's weather-vane;
The sun flings Mycenaean gold
  Against a neighbor's window-pane.

Jean Lenski

Explanation

I am less here than others. Practicing
the art of poise upon a slender ledge
that drops down days, resolving not to sing
a favorite nocturne, pruning back the edge
of dreams—all these are such consuming tasks.
And morning means that I must nurse a flame
so I can study what the daylight asks,
            and research why
            and memorize
                my name.

Philip Booth
This Dream

I climb up from this dream
the way, last fall, I finally
survived diving into a quarry:
by swimming, from dark, for
light as hard as pink granite.
They tell me I almost drowned.
Warm as I've grown, I'm
of no mind to remember.
As if from deep cold, I only know
to invite myself back: I tip
my eyes empty of sleep; then,
with the heel of each hand, I tap
the ringing out of each temple.
The small bells keep on.
If this is fever, I want it.
Everything's clear: the sun
has come back from nowhere,
and brought with it incalculable light.
This morning will not go away.
No more will I: I am in my element;
I baptize myself by breathing my name,
I give my new face to the sun.
I smile like everything, even
at me: I think I am perfectly mad:
I believe I will live forever.

Daniel Halpern
The Mole

Outside another cheery day is going on.
The gay life in the sun that breeds
the darkness that lasts into night.
I live in the continuously cheery day—
the brides are white, the air is white,
the dresses of the children are white.
I walk among so much, and touch the skin
or eyes of those in light. The days last
as long as they can, and the darkness
grows from behind the trees and houses.
So what good is so much cheer? Outside the dark
streets end in more darkness. Somewhere children
are in bright rooms with their parents.
It is night, and as I enter sleep
the last movements are going on.
This is the other part, the mole
soundless, sliding beneath me—its dark life
only movement, constant night, something long and steady,
unchanging except for the cool and the warm turning
over and over till I wake.

Marcia Southwick

The Mood Museum: *Anxiety*

The rain's nonsense-syllables are locked in my head.
Am I really alive?
I wouldn't know just by breathing.
Small things must happen to make me aware of it: gravel in my
  shoe,
or keys jingling in my pocket . . .
When the sun splits the clouds it will clarify everything
except for the shadows that bother me.
I wear the shadows like sheep's clothing.
I keep my mouth shut.
My occupation is silence and doubt.
I'm looking for a fire escape. I'm hoping to slip unnoticed
with my suitcase out into the street.
But I'm worried that the moon might spot me if I run.
My mind is revving too fast
like an engine smelling of diesel.
The rain utters its keynote address,
and tomorrow the sun will want to interview me
in its harsh light. What should I do?
My worries objectify themselves into a leak in the roof
and a broken shutter banging against the house.
I open the refrigerator and find that my sour feelings
are milk gone bad. For hours I stare at the nervous and dizzy
  trees.
Then I pull myself together, go to a party, and chat,
a white silk rose in my hair. I say, "Nice to meet you!"
My self-hatred slips into a stranger's face
and stares back at me with its steely eyes and wild black hair.
I almost say to the face, "Your ears stick out. Ever think of that?"
At home I think, *Those trees will either die or go mad.*
I wish the wind would shut up.
It rattles the window like the intrusion of unwanted advice.
It crosses over the rage line,
beating the trees with its airy fists.
Maybe a secret inside of me has translated itself

into that crow clinging to a skinny branch.
The night is stealing things: a barn here, a field there.
Maybe a flock of sheep spirals into the heavens, sucked up by Time,
and nothingness is a mechanical genius.
Maybe Death is trying to talk me into backgammon
and will offer me a cocktail, saying, "Here, have a disease."
My glance drifting across the wallpaper
washes the floral designs with a tiny fraction of my ill will.
You asked for an explanation and all I can give you is
diagonal rain and my vintage record collection.
I can only give you forms to fill out and bills to pay.
It's God reaching down with a surgically-gloved hand
making a mess of this whole operation. I can't take it.
If the saints conducted seminars on timidity, I'd get an A.
The sky has no alternative address,
and morning will come, throwing its light
into obscure corners, undertaking the huge project
of the world's exposure. Until then, what should I do?

Peter Cooley
In the Crepuscular

You have but to lift your hand
and this time appears to you
between day lily, night star,
between cobalt, indigo.

You have but to give your word
to any name not your own
and through it floods such music
as becomes the sycamore,

the tree frog's obligato
skrete of cricket, the oboe
from locusts in the live oak
until this minute secret.

This is the hour of gold leaf
at the edge of your pages,
when assuming beak and claw
you take off on sudden wing,

answering cries of women
calling you to them, rising,
the honey of each moment
you imagine as you come.

You have but to lift your palm
to see how finely written,
how minute the continents
between little finger, thumb,

you to whom fire is given
for song and so intensely
you must renounce it lightly
when the darkness takes your hand.

Liz Rosenberg

New Days

Sunlight, strong as
tobacco, that shines
so hard it seems

to push the door
ajar just as
you and I

leaned into a kiss, reached
under clothes to find our
skins. Bright earth,

forgive this
darkness
working in me.

Harvey Shapiro
Days and Nights

I.

You keep beating me down.
When I reach a balance,
You break it, always
Clawing for the heart.
In the electric light
We face each other.
Whatever you want of me,
Goddess of insomnia and pure form,
It's not these messages I scratch out
Morning after morning
To turn you off.

2.

Whether I had room
For all that joy
In my economy
Is another matter.
Rejecting me,
She shut out all my light,
Showed to me the backs
Of houses, tail lights
Going fast,
Smiles disappearing.
Every man
Was my enemy.
So it was for many a day.
I could not
Climb out of it,
So close was I
To her will.

3.

"He that is wise may correct natures."
Alchemy. The philosophical stone.
Your shadow over the page.
Your hair to my cheek.
Your eyes great riding lights
In the alcoholic storm that now
I remember, along with that
Bruising sweat of rhetoric
I thought appropriate to the times.
He that is wise
May have his life to remember.
But I am reduced to reciting
The letters of the alphabet.
If I say them with fervor
(Saying them with fervor)
Will memory be stirred?
Your own goddess-voice
In the leaves, in the night
Of the body, as I turn the page.

4.

Well, it was only Bottom's dream—
Methought I was and
Methought I had.
Outside, the sky is a field
In which the seeds of minerals shine.
And I am hunched over the board
On which I write my nights
Breathing configurations
On the winter air. As far from you
As ever I was from you.
The cold locks everything in place.
Now I am here. The flame of my match
Everything that is given to me.

5.

Suddenly I see your face close up
And all my senses scramble
To get the shock
Home again. In sleep
Not knowing who I am
Or however that spent match struck.

6.

The white brilliance under the eyelids
So that all things appear to me
In that color. The worlds you see
Exist in joy. Eyes like doves.
Equilibrium, a white brilliance.

7.

Now you come again
Like a very patient ghost,
Offering me Zen records,
A discourse on the stomach
As the seat of the soul,
Your long white neck to kiss.
The tiger's eye that is
Your favorite jewel
Shines in your hand.
Wanting to, I can't conjure
You up, not a touch.
Unbidden, you cross a thousand miles
To say, This is the gift
I was going to give you forever.

Marcia Southwick
The Mood Museum: *Sloth & Torpor*

I won't get up. Not until morning stops this uncertain
giddiness and settles for a more straightforward daylight.
Somewhere, Death is rattling in its box, shaking with music.
Am I there too, materializing as a high, shrill note?
I'm at home with language in its big room of phrases,
but I'm also afraid that its subtle inferences might kill me.
What I mean to say is that the light's fervent impulses
are wasted on me. Or the night, seeking its private revenge,
won't let morning heal the breach made by the absence of light.
There are certain pockets of air in which my sadness
has become invisible matter nevertheless contained
by the intake of breath. I've given my replies.
I've named my silences. But what are their names?
How can I be expected to know when I haven't been informed
by the Big Blaze, the irrational occasion for the first pulse,
the first breath? We're here by accident—this morning
is giving me a lethal doily,
the sky at noon won't look at me anymore with such horror
that I will see myself as one of its major impediments.
I don't regard the sky as my chosen audience. I'd rather
address a substitute that isn't so wracked by useless grief.
Everywhere I look, the walls of flame aren't there.
And I don't know why. My friend, excuse me.
I've counted clouds until I've gone blind in this dream
of staying alive in a place where everything
is put into question, even this voice—this voice of whatever I was
before I was born under the sign of a different logic, a different
    light.

Michael Pettit
Bewildering Miracle

A kind of euphoria follows pain,
like, after weeping all night, you can't help
but grow giddy at dawn—all that clear light,
all those long shadows you find so lovely
when only hours before, nothing was.
What metamorphic spirit, world of change.

Say one bad morning you have your failures
in line—no good now, or then, or to come.
Say you are low low low, down deep and damn,
from somewhere, come these annoying *noises*
to disturb you, to threaten your breakfast
depression. Go away. No, not noises—

you hear, what?, notes of *music* come floating,
broken by the clear, cold, early March wind.
And they grow louder, more insistent, more
coherent—fractured sounds now one sound
coming closer. *Band* music? Yes, by damn,
a band coming down your street, toward you.

It is not yet seven in the morning,
cold, and you are in a bad way, alone,
but here comes this marching band, boys and girls
in school clothes and coats, in strict formation,
playing some Sousa tune—crisp, bright, lively.
You leave the window, walk outside to watch

the parade pass: three snapping flags first,
troop of cute baton twirlers, then the band—
fifes and flutes, gold trumpets, trombones, tubas,
snare and kettle drums, xylophone, cymbals—
fifty, maybe sixty musicians, all
playing in tune, marching along in step.

You stand on your stoop, you look and listen—
sun flashing off brass horns, pink faces lit,
cold breaths rising with the Sousa, caught there,
released, going as they go, down the street,
around a corner, the music fading,
breaking up again, brisk March air bearing

one last high note, one last drum roll to you,
standing alone now, stunned, feeling both full
and at a loss to say what just took place.
An illusion? You were sure all parades
were over forever, and now this, this
bright, *con brio*, bewildering miracle.

Lawson Fusao Inada
Don't Know

Don't know what's come over me:
like to keep covered up—
flappy caps, and turn away from lights . . .

Thought I was getting somewhere—
the lofty perspective, repose . . .

Here we goes again.

Each morning, cornered by your clicking pens,
I'm the Prince of Articulates
hiccuping in a confessional—

eyes, eyes, eyes . . .

And when mechanics, those
lewd pryers, lift my hood and leer,
I keep my knees closed—

tight, tight . . .

And last night I knew it wasn't right

and I laughed and laughed until I cried.

Marcia Southwick

The Mood Museum: *Depression*

A knock at the door, and there it was—Depression,
the corners of its mouth turned down in disapproval.
I said, "Excuse me. I've got dishes to do.
If you want to borrow something, a cup
of doubt or agony, you'll have to go elsewhere."
And it said, "If you think you can get away without noticing
the little black patches of shadow everywhere, you're mistaken.
You can either officially quit living, or I'll fire you.
You can suffer my condition marked by irreversible
mental deterioration, or you will forever be banished by the stars.
Would you rather shed your image and look more like me,
or become invisible so that you can see through yourself?"
"Go away," I said. The next day it was back.
"Already the voices inside you are cancelling each other out,"
   it said.
"Even though you're making an effort to look innocent,
you are corrupted by waves of envy and nausea.
Fear and dread are rooting themselves at the base of your skull."
The next day, its pain was still with me, like a last note vibrating
on the strings of a harp. An anxiety serving no purpose
shuttled back and forth between my childhood and adulthood.
I was the inventor of misguided thoughts. I gazed
into my own interior, memorizing details—tables set for one,
and nothing but candles for illumination. I worried
that even the gray rain would leave me, due to its private set
of convictions. Maybe the sky had an airy, uncluttered look
because it was dreaming of my absence. I needed help.
I was an idle onlooker, while all around me flowers and trees
were giving me suspicious looks. Were the saints applauding
my madness? The stars didn't owe me anything,
yet I kept feeling that they should pay me back. But for what?
I stood naked in front of the mirror so long that I saw
what I looked like before I was born: I was invisible,
like an accumulation of messages passing briefly through DNA,

a shadow passing through my parents' ability to get on each
    other's nerves,
or a gesture that hadn't yet expressed itself in terms of someone's
    hands.
I'm wondering, why do the unborn cross the existential divide
    into life,
breaking away from the oneness of light? Don't they know
that death will later retrieve them? Let me stay. Let me live here
in the wake of this starlight that will never forgive me!

Tino Villanueva

Again

So I depend again upon myself.
I've taught this part of me
to go unruined
through all enormous lessons
on defeat.
I've taught this part of me
to thrive among despair,
to be imperative
among chaotic numbers.
Though I may fall away from time to time
like draggled weeds in winter,
breathing thick stern air
in some back shadows of the walk,
I spring again from me,
from the dead quiet of my roots—
listen to me move.

By dawn
I am presence fixed
in the eyes of men.

Leo Connellan

Helpless, We Go Into This Ground, Helpless

Across the bridges and under the earth,
subway trains lumber and clank.

Helpless, we go into this ground, helpless
each day packed against each other so that
we always start off irritable
at being tossed about, thrown against strangers.

People who never get to know each other
but ride the train every day
without ever exchanging dreams.

The subway screeches
ear-piercingly through tunnels
and rattles into the station
like an undone accordion.

The whole subway train shudders
as it stops. The train doors
open like gasping mouths.

And we get on staggering
shadows of giants forced
to become Subway Passengers
pushing, shoving, we are made
into something else than human
in this insult cramming against each
other in our own foul exhale.

In the subway water
always falling off
station walls as though
the held-back rivers
will break through over us.

Here we are flushed out
of our anonymity.

        To whom do we look good?
        Villon, did you do that!

We get on the same train
every morning for years
and usually the same car.

        Through the earth and on the bridges
        subway trains groan . . .

We get off the train
and go a hundred
different directions
to our daily fates.

We get on the same train
every morning, surviving
the subway each day as
prisoners do, disassociating
from what was . . . and is . . .
and will be . . .

        But, Subways I
        defeated you.

        Overwhelming Subways I
        hung on.

I climbed, climbed, climbed
your endless straight-up
stairs back out to sunshine.

Helpless, we go into this ground, helpless
onto dank dark brutally cold
impartial platforms to wait
for trains that throw our insides around

until panic seizes and you gasp
in terror that you might suffocate,
with the scribblings of restrained
psychotics on everything, the walls, posts,
train windows, all over the trains in
insulting thumbed noses at us, vulgar orange, purple
which the rest of unstable us who somehow
cope must add to what we endure. We
let them draw on us rather than slaughter us.

But there is no such help for us,
if we suddenly blow it's Bellevue
or one of those unfortunate assassinations
by the good-guy off-duty cop who just happened
to be on his way home with a well-loaded gun ready
for us because we aren't ghetto kids
in the amnesty of invisible veiled threat to
go wild in our condition.

We go helpless down into this ground, helpless.
Can you imagine getting stalled underground,
the subway train coming to a full stop down
deep in the earth in ninety-nine-degree heat,
the train stops and the sickening
scent of burning wood . . .

        Off the bridges and into the earth
        gouged out for it the subway train stalls.

Helpless, down in the ground, we are under
the earth now in company of people we don't
know . . . helpless into this ground, helpless.

We have resigned ourselves wrecks to them
these shattering, jarring subway trains that
we must take or not go anywhere.

WITH THE SEASONS

Hayden Carruth

Depression

The cells of one's body renew themselves every
     seven years—is that right? And so does one's
depression, yes, every seven years, lifelong. This fall
     the foliage has turned earlier than usual, the wind
has been stronger, the rain stronger, and the leaves
     are wet and brown on the soaked earth. Yes-
terday we heard, still in September, and quickly saw
     a small flock of geese overhead going westward,
their discourse wordy in the sky. One bird was far
     ahead of the rest, and the rest were a ragged flight,
as if they were desperate, stumbling, unable
     to form a proper community, arguing. But they
were still the first geese of the new season, wondrous
     to us. My dear, I wish our controversy were
as comely. Where are we going, so ragged and hasty?
     We have tried hard, have labored against the seasons
like the geese, year after year, against mania, fear,
     depression, death in the heart, the endless mockery
of the children in our minds, we have hurled fat insults
     at each other, have hurled silence, the same
occult and cloudy words over and over in the wet
     wind, we have persisted, tattered and worn out
and sorry. Thank God we love each other and can hold
     our tongues and go to bed, otherwise this
would be intolerable, traveling so far, so long, and never
     arriving anywhere. Nor do the geese. Nor the seasons.

Cynthia Huntington
There

These woods have no memory and do not end,
indistinct beyond the black tendons of pines
that twist upward into the air, holding themselves still.
Beyond, all blank and quiet now
snow falls straight down, no wind, almost
nothing moving, and I stand here nowhere staring
into the white space of everything that happens.
Grass and weeds stick through the pond's ice
like stubble in an open field, where once in Michigan
I stood at dusk. Black birds flew past me,
rising and falling, toward the far trees—
flew past me like a stone, or a shadow on the ground.
They seemed like something torn out of the earth,
its naked furrows broken at my feet. Behind me, windows
opened bright eyes at evening. I would not go back.

It's nearly dark now; snow surrounds me, forms
repeat and don't repeat, touching everything at once.
I want to stay here, like staying inside a memory
of a bad time, that is no longer painful. Now I see
how beautiful the trees always were,
the deep, responsive peace among them,
and tangled lines of cat-brier knotting
the world together, the muscular beauty of hills
and deep tracks some dog made running sideways along the ridge.

A jay, dull in snow-light, rattling branches overhead,
seems to call back every living thing I looked at
once, through a narrow window of sorrow
in a winter before he lived, when another
season's birds threw themselves hungrily into the sky.
It was not sorrow, but rage that slid over me like ice,
then, sealing the world in perfect, silent cold.
I was still, and in me nothing moved,

yet the seasons carried me with them, turned me
back and forward again, so I moved inside the years.

This storm began over the Great Lakes and traveled east;
it was in Michigan three days ago and kept on
to this coast where every weather ends, where storms
are lost at sea. I am here; I am lost.
And if, far back in Michigan, another storm falls into evening,
may I stand in another life? I would not go back.
That jay, flying off after some new
desire of his own, has been flying away from me for years—
generous messenger among the downward-drifting bodies,
hurrying though none will be saved. Don't stop,
I am telling him. I am here; I will be there soon,
where you are going.

Carol Lem

Something Is There

It moves so slowly
this hand shaping a phrase
I can come back to these winter mornings
when all there is are these stale images to recycle
because the heart doesn't know
when it's had enough.
Last night I dreamt of the old house
my room stacked with dusty boxes . . .
if only I had time to sort them out
but I'm going to die
without knowing what's inside,
if only I could remember
what filled them in the first place.

I empty one life into another
counting tracks I've taken
how they lead to this place by the window
forcing one word into another
to make lines I must follow to the end
not knowing why.
Sixteen years I've listened to the train go by,
someday I'd like to jump it
to see where it goes
and how the old baggage comes back
illuminating shadows who follow me
from page to page

Where all the lives gather
like a cat scratching for release
blacks out, kicks against tight corners
falls to his side until the world
slowly returns to order
and each life sorts itself out
in private despair.

The heart cries no more, no more
and the body surrenders to one life
curled at the edge of the bed
in the blank stillness that comes after seizure.
Only then do words crawl on the page
with a lightness of being.

And it is morning again
with me at the desk
in the gray stillness
watching for the first bird
to emerge from the dark cypress.
Something is there
even if I don't see it.

Sandra Agricola

Paperweight: The State I'm In

My life had become unmanageable.
Which step is this?
The one we repeat every year.
Exposition Universelle.
This hollow ball
of murky depth.
My commemorative life.
Every season my days turn cobalt blue.
Meerschaum, sand and rice
fall all around me.
How to solve this problem of blue
alternating mess of mania.
Snow gone wild, helter skelter
swirling swirls.
Where is the geometric proof?
What is the cloudy message of depression?
My snowstorms are exquisite,
but I am trapped here beside Iwo Jima and Popeye,
a freestanding wonder,
a miracle under glass,
a drama that arises from within.
There is no out-of-bounds.

Jane Flanders
Stasis

Something out there
refuses to give up.

Always air rises
into the blue or gray
or heliotrope.

A leaf shuffles
across the street.

Under the ice
the pond streams and stirs.

This nameless season
that grips us from within

is far colder, darker,
very still.

Jane Kenyon
Depression in Winter

There comes a little space between the south
side of a boulder
and the snow that fills the woods around it.
Sun heats the stone, reveals
a crescent of bare ground: brown ferns,
and tufts of needles like red hair,
acorns, a patch of moss, bright green . . .

I sank with every step up to my knees,
throwing myself forward with a violence
of effort, greedy for unhappiness—
until by accident I found the stone,
with its secret porch of heat and light,
where something small could luxuriate, then
turned back down my path, chastened and calm.

Susan Ludvigson
Grief

Imagine that pure
melting of snow in Wisconsin
so that when it's gone, the earth
underneath is raw and damp,
needing sun, seed, any kind
of promise. But more snow comes
before the final thaw,
and this goes on, over and over,
so that in February, March,
you think the world may never
be green.
When you look out the picture window,
after your spirits have risen one last
slow time, old grass looks
as if it might leap to life.
Then you see those large flakes
floating down, and you weep,
past belief. It can happen
through April, hope going white
and silent again.

Michael Pettit

Fat Tuesday

Does not the heart live off light?
Beat not in the dark but send this
fiery parade winding through us?

In my blood are those old celebrations
each year from Epiphany to Lent—
balls for the rich, parades for everyone,

good times hard now, in this night,
to believe. Like then I wait, impatient
for the least first sign—distant

siren, flashing yellow lights, stirring
of the crowd lining the wide avenue, looking,
pointing, their hearts *at last!* drumming.

Brian Swann
Bipolar

The drums of foliage start up.
   Night itself catches fire.
In this kind of Alaskan spring kids
   tumble over tall tombs,
ravines stand bolt upright.
   Daybreak is never worse
than a series of lifelike pictures
   in which for the first time
the earth comes to pass.
   Satellites uncouple and go
flashing about the sky,
   eating up what cannot escape—
the sun, erotic pulp, piledriver,
   makes a final fatal jump.

The sea runs out of the courtyard
   leaving a tundra of shining stone.
The world won't stay anywhere,
   crumbling into its pit.
Birds perch on the backs of benches
   like dead souls, and the sleep
of the living shakes loose
   from the fouled headwater,
floats in moonless tides.

William Hathaway
Grief in Early Spring

March again. We thaw again.

Snowheaps speckled with grit ooze
from under gray lips of ice. All sucks
and gurgles under step. Old dog feces
poke out fresh daily, still bright
and firm as new in ice-banks—
like neolithic families they find
huddled in crypts, preserved for us
by some fortuitous, steady drips.

Branches torn down by last month's
ice storm claw out of the park meadow
like huge talons. A futile raking,
as if a stiff beak gapes below . . .

Today, brooding beside my ghost
in the window pane, I watched too
long the sparrow's fidget
along bare lilac limbs until my wits
scattered to their twiggy nerve-ends.
Each thought finally clasped
tight to a separate perch, twittering
in a stiff, monotonous swaying—
as if tugged by the enormous black
spaces always between brightnesses.

Birds don't read omens. Sap quickens
under their frenetic claspings;
claws feel all their tiny minds know.
Scient omnium, yet drab cheeping tells
nothing. You might say a merry chuckle
in the storm drains is the sun's
laughter, still sparkling bright
in black tunnels. Say what you wish
to read an earnest truth in beauty.

Because his hand's last tremble
still flutters in my hand, then
in my mind, this morning, the cheers
of that cardinal greeting sunrise
from the highest treetop melt
deeper with each scalding trill.
So bright and firm! Such stupid,
stupid hope! Coffee nerves, you say?
Right. Who'd clamber down a pipe,
forsaking sunlight and song
into echoing tar black rot-drip,
to pull back up the beloved dead?

Elspeth Cameron Ritchie

Spring Lettuce

When the March wind tossed sandy Maryland,
When the osprey began to dive for sticks,
When jellyfish floated in, their wombs red,
We planted the first black seeds.

The city was closed, rain leashing
The hospital in tethers of traffic.
Patients played cards, smoked, dreamed.
I stayed late, dictating charts.

Radishes burst first, tearing up to the sun.
Timidly the lettuce peeked to spy on
The fanfarewell of the geese, and duck at
Shotgun shells raking from dead blinds.

Mad men and women flew in from Europe,
Lashed to gurneys, legs twitching,
Minds aswarm, families left, souls beaten.
We helped them up, switched their meds.

Time to plant feathery dill and fetid cilantro,
But the purple basil failed of cold.
Starflowers thrust through the antique grass.
Tractors flung the furrows wide.

A man put a plastic bag over his head and died
In a froth of vomit. We could not revive him.
Police came. Cameras flashed.
Patients cried. I clamped down. Work to do.

White and red radishes fill the fridge.
Time for tomatoes, tamped down with dung.
Tears finally came, as the cages went
Around the stalks. How could you suicide in spring?

The inquest ended. No negligence.
Patients found their clothes, called their wives.
Volleyballs pounded the office windows.
A nurse announced. Baby showers.

Now the ospreys tend their eggs
In the locust leaning over the tide.
Underneath sound the thwocks of croquet balls.
We dug the sailboat from the sand.

A woman with AIDS lost her unborn child.
She asked me whether he would go to heaven
Or hell, since he was tainted. I replied,
Heaven, I think. She, too, wants to die.

A hundred head of lettuce extrude.
Spinach has gone to seed. Girls glide
On the beach. I read Freud.
Black men plant tobacco by hand.

Time for me to leave the ward.
Cocaine addicts revolve through the doors.
I feed the staff bread and lettuce.
Turkey vultures roost in the barn.

The baby jellyfish gather offshore.
Boundaries of ward and garden fade.
Worms swarm in both. I weed and fertilize.
Sails fly, frantically, through the river.

David Budbill
The End of Winter

The delicate and lovely emptiness of winter
  gone now today, suddenly gone,
    this last week
      of May.

The glut of summer rushes in,
  grass crowding everything,
    trees thick again
      with green.

The whole world full of life and noise
  closing in, and nowhere for us
    dark ones, depressed ones,
      to hide.

Miriam Dyak
Mania

Woman   this is the seventeenth potion
      I have brewed to snare you
Its aroma steams from your mother's nightgown
      from pepper blossoms in the summer garden
It is sweet as an all-day sucker
      and bites like the virgin in your dreams

This whole orange season
      I have felt suddenly sad
I swallow our ecstasy whole   each night
      in a capsule
When you make love to me   I fly out
      onto mountains
A clear day I can see the sea   and you
      a purple dot   blinking in and out on the horizon
We still touch   a long note on an elastic string of time
We laugh   at our own miracles

I laugh and the frosts twist in my womb like scissors
My shoulders come apart and will not refit together
I pace   You are gone
I am tall as the ceiling
My ten-league boots devour these two small rooms
      like stale crumbs
I throw frayed darts and leave
      one bull's-eye to watch for your return

Linda Pastan

Hurricane Watch

I saw once,
through the eyepiece of a microscope,
a blizzard of cells.
And at times
the hairs on my arm lift,
as if in some incalculable wind,
or my throat echoes
the first hoarse forecast
of thunder.
Some live in the storm's eye only.
I rise and fall
with the barometer,
holding on for my life.
Here, in a storm cellar
of flesh,
pale as the roots I live on,
I read my palm
as though it were a weather map
and keep a hurricane watch
all year.

Shiela Cowing
Vegetable Garden After Too Much Rain

All year you long for this full measure.
Last week, these plants were poised
on the lip of fruiting, bold, inevitable.
But in this hopeless affluence
gold melons smell, tomatoes seep.
The summer weighs too much; it wakes

your old fever dream: in that black, webbed corner
near the eaves, every mucous pore
dried out except the eyes, which run,
you're too gross to fit between rafters,
you must be stuffed. The season's flatulent,
the squash furry, gooey-stemmed.

Ira Sadoff

Depression Beginning in 1956

for Jon and Barbara

This mood's not mirrored in the weather, raining,
nor can it be cured
by the usual remedies. It is a mood, unlike the geography
of rivers, without a source, all too general,
like a conversation with a stranger, a way of living
you've adjusted to. Only you haven't
shaken the feeling something's wrong, your wife is off
with someone else, or you would like to be.

Your father sitting in a chair one July is a thought
you have now, in a time before air conditioners, sweating
through his shirt. You think you know what he is thinking:
should he buy a new house, get a divorce,
should he vote for a Democrat who has no chance to win,
should he help your mother in the kitchen though he doesn't
want to see her again? He's not sitting in that chair now
so he must have moved. Or something moved in him.
   The lesson
you want to learn is how we change ourselves,
how we move from past to future.

                              If we follow
the movement of flowers and trees, which we don't, we would
    know
it's not through consciousness—the lilac
that blooms at night knows nothing of that change.
Nor is it something large, what we do in the eyes
of others—what do the branches care for the leaves
when they grow up or down?

                         And yet your father
is remarried, he voted for a Democrat, he's somewhere
else in Arizona, free of trees, at last something good

is happening to him. Why couldn't it be your mood
that's changed, what would it take to remove yourself
from this feeling, this weight of the present
mood of helplessness? It is not a great disaster
that makes us change, but a straightening
of will combined with circumstance: nature
has nothing to do with it now, though it might
have in the past, when we understood the motion
of animals against trees.

                For we are not animals
now, nor could we choose to be: though we choose sometimes
the pastoral and lovely, it is never quite enough
to leave the melancholy we've come to know,
and if that mood should pass we think it was
some miracle or strength or someone else we love
coming to our aid. And we'd be wrong in part and right
in ways we can't define in love or sometimes change.

C.K. Williams
Dominion: Depression

I don't know what day or year of their secret cycle this
 blazing golden afternoon might be,
but out in the field in a shrub hundreds of pairs of locusts
 are locked in a slow sexual seizure.

Hardly more animate than the few leaves they haven't devoured,
 they seethe like a single being,
limbs, antennas, and wings all tangled together as intricately
 as a layer of neurons.

Always the neat, tight, gazeless helmet, the exoskeleton
 burnished like half-hardened glue;
always the abdomen twitched deftly under or aside, the
 skilled rider, the skillfully ridden.

One male, though, has somehow severed a leg, it sways on
 the spike of a twig like a harp:
he lunges after his female, tilts, falls; the mass horribly
 shudders, shifts, realigns.

So dense, so hard, so immersed in their terrible need to
 endure, so unlike me but like me,
why do they seem such a denial, why do I feel if I plunged
 my hand in among them I'd die?

This must be what god thinks, beholding his ignorant,
 obstinate, libidinally maniacal offspring:
wanting to stop them, to keep them from being so much an
 image of his impotence or his will.

How divided he is from his creation: even here near the
 end he sees moving towards him
a smaller, sharper, still more gleaming something, extracting
 moist matter from a skull.

No more now: he waits, his fists full of that mute, oily,
  crackling, crystalline broil,
then he feels at last the cool wingbeat of the innocent void
  moving in again over the world.

NOTES TO THE INTRODUCTION

1. Roy Porter, *Madness: A Brief History* (Oxford: Oxford University Press, 2002); Richard Burton, *The Anatomy of Melancholy: What It Is, with All the Kinds, Causes, Symptoms, Prognostics, and Several Cures of It, in Three Partitions, with Their Several Sections, Members, and Subsections, Philosophically, Medically, Historically Opened and Cut Up* (New York: Wiley, 1850 [1621]).

2. See the American Psychiatric Association, *Diagnostic and Statistical Manual of Mental Disorders: DSM-IV-TR* (Washington, D.C.: American Psychiatric Association, 2000), xxiv–xxvii.

3. Innumerable works explore these issues, which extend into the political, legal, and economic realms and are constantly being reevaluated. For a detailed survey of competing arguments, see, for example, John Z. Sadler, *Values and Psychiatric Diagnosis* (Oxford: Oxford University Press, 2005), esp. chap. 3, "Science and Psychiatric Nosology," chap. 5, "Space, Time and Being," and chap. 7, "Culture."

4. The conflict between social and medical models has been the subject of much discussion. Critical philosophical and sociological works include Thomas S. Szasz, *The Myth of Mental Illness* (New York: Harper & Row, 1961); Michel Foucault, *Madness and Civilization: A History of Insanity in the Age of Reason* (New York: Pantheon Books, 1965); and Allan V. Horwitz, *The Social Control of Mental Illness* (New York: Academic Press, 1982). One alternative to the strictly social and medical models is the biopsychosocial model, which considers the interaction of biological, psychological, and social factors in disorder.

5. For perspectives on the role of mental disorders and creativity in evolution, see Daniel Nettle, *Strong Imagination: Madness, Cre-*

ativity and Human Nature (Oxford: Oxford University Press, 2001), 101–9, 137–60; and Dean Keith Simonton, *Origins of Genius* (New York: Oxford University Press, 1999), esp. chap. 3, "Variation: Is Genius Brilliant—or Mad?"

6. In Plato, divine madness is distinguished from human madness, however. Plato, "Phaedrus," in *The Dialogues of Plato*, trans. Benjamin Jowett (New York: Oxford University Press, 1892), 1:449–51; and see also Plato, "Ion" (ibid., 1: 501–3).

7. Nancy C. Andreasen, "Creativity and Mental Illness: Prevalence Rates in Writers and Their First-Degree Relatives," *American Journal of Psychiatry* 144 (October 1987): 1288–92.

8. Kay Redfield Jamison, *Touched with Fire: Manic-Depressive Illness and the Artistic Temperament* (New York: Free Press, 1993).

9. Arnold M. Ludwig, *The Price of Greatness: Resolving the Creativity and Madness Controversy* (New York: Guilford Press, 1995).

10. For Rothenberg's criticism of specific research methods, see *Creativity and Madness: New Findings and Old Stereotypes* (Baltimore: Johns Hopkins University Press, 1990), esp. 80–89, and 149–150; letters to the editor, *American Journal of Psychiatry* 152 (May 1995): 815–16; and "Bipolar Illness, Creativity, and Treatment," *Psychiatric Quarterly* 72 (June 2001: 131–47. Rothenberg is not the only critic of these methods. See also the citations in note 12.

11. John Cody, *After Great Pain: The Inner Life of Emily Dickinson* (Cambridge, MA: Belknap Press of Harvard University Press, 1971); Eleanor Ruggles, *The West-Going Heart: A Life of Vachel Lindsay* (New York: Norton, 1959); Allan Seager, *The Glass House: The Life of Theodore Roethke* (Ann Arbor: University of Michigan Press, 1991); James Atlas, *Delmore Schwartz: The Life of an American Poet* (New York: Farrar, Straus and Giroux, 1971); Paul L. Mariani, *Dream Song: The Life of John Berryman* (New York: Morrow, 1990); William H. Pritchard, *Randall Jarrell: A Literary Life* (New York: Farrar, Straus and Giroux, 1990); Diane Wood Middlebrook, *Anne Sexton: A Biography* (Boston: Houghton Mifflin, 1991); Ian Hamilton, *Robert Lowell: A Biography* (New York: Random House, 1982); and Anne Stevenson, *Bitter Fame: A Life of Sylvia Plath* (Boston: Houghton Mifflin, 1989).

12. For a critical review of the scientific evidence for associating creativity and mental illness, see Charlotte Waddell, "Creativity

and Mental Illness: Is There a Link?" *Canadian Journal of Psychiatry* 43 (March 1998): 166-72. See also Nettle, *Strong Imagination*, 142–44; Dean Keith Simonton, *Greatness: Who Makes History and Why* (New York: Guilford Press, 1994), 286–90; and the works cited in note 10. Simonton says, "The human mind is not very adept at drawing valid qualitative inferences from data as complex as those found in the historical record" ("Qualitative and Quantitative Analyses of Historical Data," in *Annual Review of Psychology*, vol. 54, ed. Susan T. Fiske [Palo Alto: Annual Reviews, 2003], p. 628).

13. See, for example, Simonton, *Origins of Genius*, 75–107; Simonton, *Greatness*, esp. chap. 10, "The Significance of Psychopathology"; Jamison, *Touched with Fire*, esp. chap. 3, "Could It Be Madness—This?"; Ludwig, *Price of Greatness*; Albert Rothenberg, *The Emerging Goddess: The Creative Process in Art, Science, and Other Fields* (Chicago: University of Chicago Press, 1979); Rothenberg, *Creativity and Madness*; and Frank Barron, *Creativity and Psychological Health: Origins of Personal Vitality and Creative Freedom* (New York: D. Van Nostrand Company, 1963). See also Kenneth Rexroth, "The Vivisection of a Poet," *The Nation*, December 14, 1957: 450–53, for a vivid commentary on psychological studies of poets. Definitions of creativity and genius vary widely and have generated substantial controversy.

14. For a consideration of prominent Romantic-era distinctions between talent and genius and an in-depth analysis of Romantic thought on the relationship between madness and poetry, see Frederick Burwick, *Poetic Madness and the Romantic Imagination* (University Park: Pennsylvania State University Press, 1996), esp. chap. 1, "Genius, Madness, and Inspiration."

15. See Simonton, *Greatness*, 138–41; Simonton, *Origins of Genius*, 90–92; Rothenberg, *Creativity and Madness*, 9; Jamison, *Touched with Fire*, 97; and Barron, *Creativity and Psychological Health*, chap. 19, "The Creative Writer." For an overview of research that addresses the impact of positive and negative affects on creativity, see *Affect, Creative Experience, and Psychological Adjustment*, ed. Sandra W. Russ (Philadelphia: Brunner/Mazel, 1999). In Waddell's assessment, "Enthusiasm for associating creativity and mental illness exceeds the scientific evidence and persists despite

evidence to the contrary" ("Creativity and Mental Illness: Is There a Link?" 170).

16. Charles Lamb, "Sanity of True Genius," in *The Works of Charles and Mary Lamb*, ed. E. V. Lucas (London: Methuen and Company, 1903), 2:187. (Lamb's essay was originally published in the May 1826 issue of *New Monthly Magazine*, pp. 519–20, under the title "That great Wit is allied to Madness.") Wilhelm Dilthey agreed: "Only the healthy imagination is capable of organizing images and impressions into a work of art" ("Dichterische Einbildungskraft und Wahnsinn" [1866], in *Gesammelte Schriften*, vol. 6, ed. Georg Misch [Leipzig and Berlin: B.G. Teubner, 1924], cited in Burwick, *Poetic Madness and the Romantic Imagination*, 14).

17. "Mood" is cognate with, among others: Old Frisian *mōd*, disposition, feeling, mind, courage, will, intention; West Frisian *moed*, courage, hope, zest for life; Dutch *moed*, courage, conviction, heart, spirit, nerve; Old Saxon *mōd*, conviction, courage, mind, heart; Middle High German *muot*, faculty of thought, feeling, will, understanding, soul, spirit, disposition, emotion, arrogance, desire, conviction, hope, courage; and Old Danish *mod*, courage, sense, convictions. In archaic usage, the word included the meanings: "1. Mind, thought, will. Also: heart, feeling. *Obs.*, 2. a. Fierce courage; spirit, vigour. Also: pride, arrogance. *Obs.* b. Anger, wrath. c. Passionate grief. *Obs.*" *OED Online*, s.v. "mood, n.1"(http://dictionary.oed.com/cgi/entry/00315320; accessed April 14, 2007).

18. See, for instance, John Berryman, interview by Peter A. Stitt, July 1970, in *Writers at Work: The Paris Review Interviews*, ed. George Plimpton, 4th series (New York: Viking Press, 1976), 322. "Certain great artists can make out without it . . . but mostly you need ordeal," Berryman commented, although, soon after saying this, he reflected, "I'm sure this is a preposterous attitude, but I'm not ashamed of it"—and then, following the interview, he annotated this statement with a single word: "Delusion."

19. See Anne Sexton to Frederick Morgan, May 6, 1960, in *Anne Sexton: A Self-Portrait in Letters*, ed. Linda Gray Sexton and Lois Ames (Boston: Houghton Mifflin Company, 1977), 105; and Denise Levertov, "Anne Sexton: Light Up the Cave," in *Light Up the Cave* (New York: New Directions, 1981), 83–84.

20. The more complete statement is: "Poetry is the spontaneous overflow of powerful feelings; it takes its origin from emotion recollected in tranquillity: the emotion is contemplated till, by a species of reaction, the tranquility gradually disappears, and an emotion, kindred to that which was before the subject of contemplation, is gradually produced, and does itself actually exist in the mind. In this mood successful composition generally begins, and in a mood similar to this it is carried on; but the emotion, of whatever kind and in whatever degree, from various causes, is qualified by various pleasures, so that in describing any passions whatsoever, which are voluntarily described, the mind will, upon the whole, be in a state of enjoyment." See William Wordsworth, *Lyrical Ballads* (Philadelphia: James Humphries, 1802), viii.

21. Rothenberg, *Creativity and Madness*, 11–37. For additional discussion of positive cognitive functioning in creative individuals, see Rothenberg's *The Emerging Goddess* and the other citations in note 15.

22. Levertov, *Light Up the Cave*, 81.

23. William Stafford, interview by Irv Broughton, in *The Writer's Mind: Interviews with American Authors*, ed. Irv Broughton (Fayetteville: University of Arkansas Press, 1989), 1:357–58.

24. Edwin Muir, "Poetry and the Poet," in *The Estate of Poetry* (Cambridge, MA: Harvard University Press. 1962), 81.

Sandra Agricola is the author of three books of poetry: *Yellow* (Mercy Seat Press, 2004), *White Mercedes* (Ohio Review Books, 1988), and *Master Bedroom Poems* (Ohio Review Books, 1985). Her poems have appeared in many journals, including *The Georgia Review*, *Denver Quarterly*, and *The Ohio Review*.

Dick Allen's sixth poetry collection is *The Day Before: New Poems* (Sarabande Books, 2003). Sarabande Books also published his *Ode to the Cold War: Poems New and Selected* (1997) and will publish his *Clatter of a Broken Title: Newest Poems* in 2008. His work has appeared in the *Pushcart Prize* and *Best American Poetry* anthologies, *The New Yorker*, *The Hudson Review*, *The Atlantic Monthly*, and *Poetry*.

David Baker's recent books are *Radiant Lyre: Essays on Lyric Poetry* (Graywolf Press, 2007) and *Midwest Eclogue* (W. W. Norton, 2005). He is poetry editor of *The Kenyon Review*.

Angela Ball received the 2006 Donald Hall Prize in Poetry for *Night Clerk in the Hotel of Both Worlds* (University of Pittsburgh Press, 2007). Her other books of poetry include *The Museum of the Revolution: 58 Exhibits* (Carnegie Mellon University Press, 1999), *Quartet* (Carnegie Mellon University Press, 1995), *Possession* (Red Hen Press, 1995), and *Kneeling Between Parked Cars* (Owl Creek Press, 1990). She teaches in the Center for Writers at the University of Southern Mississippi, in Hattiesburg.

Gerald Barrax is the author of *From a Person Sitting in Darkness: New and Selected Poems* (Louisiana State University Press, 1998), *Leaning Against the Sun* (University of Arkansas Press, 1992), *Epigraphs* (Mud

Puppy Press, 1990), *The Deaths of Animals and Lesser Gods* (University of Kentucky Press, 1984), *An Audience of One* (University of Georgia Press, 1980), and *Another Kind of Rain* (University of Pittsburgh Press, 1970). He lives in Raleigh, North Carolina.

Linda Bierds's seventh book of poetry, *First Hand* (Putnam), was published in 2005 and was selected as a Notable Book by the American Library Association. She teaches at the University of Washington and in 1998 was named a fellow of the MacArthur Foundation.

Chana Bloch is the author of three volumes of poetry: *Mrs. Dumpty* (University of Wisconsin Press, 1998), *The Past Keeps Changing* (Sheep Meadow Press, 1992), and *The Secrets of the Tribe* (Sheep Meadow Press, 1980). She has published translations of the biblical *Song of Songs* and the work of Israeli poets Yehuda Amichai and Dahlia Ravikovitch, in addition to a critical study of George Herbert.

Michael Blumenthal is the author of the memoir *All My Mothers and Fathers* (HarperCollins, 2002) and *Dusty Angel* (BOA Editions, 1999), his sixth book of poetry, as well as a collection of essays, *When History Enters the House* (Pleasure Boat Studio, 1997), and a novel, *Weinstock Among the Dying* (Zoland Books, 1993). He has been a Fulbright fellow and has taught at universities in Hungary, Israel, Germany, and France. He currently teaches at Old Dominion University, in Norfolk, Virginia.

Philip Booth (1925–2007) published many books of poetry in his lifetime, including *Lifelines: Selected Poems, 1950–1999* (Viking Press, 1999) and *Pairs* (1994). He has been honored by fellowships from the Guggenheim Foundation, the Rockefeller Foundation, and the National Endowment for the Arts.

Carole Ann Borges is the author of *Disciplining the Devil's Country* (Alice James Books, 1987). Her poems have appeared in a number of literary magazines, including *Poetry*, *Kalliope*, *Bardsong*, and *Soundings East*. She is a reporter for the *Enlightener*, a small newspaper in Knoxville, Tennessee.

Edward Brash lives in Brooklyn, New York.

David Budbill's latest books of poetry are *While We've Still Got Feet* (Copper Canyon Press, 2005) and *Moment to Moment: Poems of a Mountain Recluse* (Copper Canyon Press, 1999). In 1999 Chelsea Green Publishing Company published a revised and expanded edition of *Judevine*, his collected poems.

Hayden Carruth has published numerous books, including *Toward the Distant Islands: New and Selected Poems* (Copper Canyon Press, 2006). He has received the National Book Award, the National Book Critics Circle Award, and fellowships from the National Endowment for the Arts and the Guggenheim Foundation.

Diana Chang's fourth volume of poetry, *The Mind's Amazement*, was published in 1998 by Live Poet's Society. Her first novel, *The Frontiers of Love*, originally published by Random House, was reissued by the University of Washington Press in 1994.

Leo Connellan (1928–2001) was the author of fourteen books of poetry, including *The Clear Blue Lobster-Water Country* (Harcourt Brace Jovanovich, 1985), *Crossing America* (Penmaen Press, 1976), and *Another Poet in New York* (Living Poets Press, 1975). Winner of the Shelley Memorial Award, he was poet-in-residence for Connecticut State University and Connecticut's State Poet Laureate.

Peter Cooley was born in Detroit and graduated from Shimer College, the University of Chicago, and the University of Iowa. He lives in New Orleans, where he teaches creative writing at Tulane University. Carnegie Mellon published his seventh collection of poems, *A Place Made of Starlight*, in 2003.

Sheila Cowing is the author of *Stronger in the Broken Places* (Sherman Asher, 1999), a volume of poems, in addition to award-winning works of nonfiction for children. She has received a Distinguished Artist Fellowship from the New Jersey Arts Council and a Recursos Discovery Award.

Steven Cramer is the author of *Goodbye to the Orchard* (Sarabande Books, 2004), which was named an Honor Book by the Massachusetts Center for the Book, *Dialogue for the Left and Right Hand* (Lumen Editions, 1997), *The World Book* (Copper Beech Press, 1992), and *The Eye That Desires to Look Upward* (Galileo Press, 1987). He directs the low-residency MFA program in creative writing at Lesley University, in Cambridge, Massachusetts.

Erica Dawson is the author of *Big-Eyed Afraid* (Waywiser Press, 2007). Her poems have appeared in the *Sewanee Theological Review*, the *Southwest Review*, the *Virginia Quarterly Review*, and other publications. She is the Elliston Fellow in Poetry at the University of Cincinnati.

Miriam Dyak lives in Seattle, Washington.

Jane Flanders (1940–2001) was the author of *The Students of Snow* (University of Massachusetts Press, 1982) and *Timepiece* (University of Pittsburgh Press, 1988). Two of her collections, *Sudden Plenty* and *Manifesto d'Amore*, were posthumously published by Bunny and Crocodile Press.

C. B. Follett is the author of four books of poetry, the most recent of which is *Hold and Release* (Time Being Books, 2006). She is the editor of *GRRRRR: A Collection of Poems About Bears* (Arctos Press, 1999) and co-editor and publisher of *RUNES: A Review of Poetry*.

Reginald Gibbons's most recent works of poetry are *Fern-Texts* (Hollyridge Press, 2005), *In the Warhouse* (Fractal Edge Press, 2004), and *It's Time* (Louisiana State University Press, 2002). His novel, *Sweetbitter*, originally published by Penguin Books, appeared in paperback from Lousiana State University Press in 2003. A professor of English and classics at Northwestern University, he has published translations of Spanish, Mexican, and ancient Greek poetry and drama.

Albert Goldbarth lives in Wichita, Kansas. His most recent books are *The Kitchen Sink: New and Selected Poems, 1972–2007* (Graywolf Press, 2007) and *Griffin* (Essay Press, 2007). Two of his collections, *Saving Lives* (Ohio State University Press, 2001) and *Heaven and Earth* (University of Georgia Press, 1991), have received the National Book Critics Circle Award.

Susan Hahn is a poet and playwright and the editor of *TriQuarterly* magazine. She is the author of seven volumes of poetry, including *The Scarlet Ibis* (Northwestern University Press, 2007), and the recipient of a Guggenheim Fellowship.

Donald Hall served as Poet Laureate of the United States from 2006 to 2007. His books of poetry include *White Apples and the Taste of Stone: Poems, 1946–2006* (Houghton Mifflin, 2006), *Without* (Houghton Mifflin, 1998), *The Museum of Clear Ideas* (Ticknor & Fields, 1993), and *The One Day* (Ticknor & Fields, 1988). He lives in New Hampshire and was married to Jane Kenyon.

Daniel Halpern's most recent book is *Something Shining* (Alfred A. Knopf, 1999). He is the publisher of Ecco, an imprint of HarperCollins.

William Hathaway's many books include *Promeneur Solitaire* (Chestercreek Press, 2005) and *Sightseer* (Canio's Editions, 2000). He lives in Surry, Maine.

Gwen Head is the author of four books of poetry, most recently *Fire Shadows* (Louisiana State University Press, 2001). The founding editor of Dragon Gate Press, she lives in Berkeley, California.

Anthony Hecht (1923–2004) published numerous books, including *Collected Later Poems* (2003), *The Darkness and the Light* (2001), *Collected Earlier Poems* (1990), and *The Transparent Man* (1990) (all from Alfred A. Knopf). After serving in the infantry during Word War II, he taught at various universities and colleges. He was awarded the Pulitzer Prize and from 1982 to 1984 served as Consultant in Poetry to the Library of Congress, the post now known as Poet Laureate.

David Hernandez's poetry collections include *Always Danger* (Southern Illinois University Press, 2006) and *A House Waiting for Music* (Tupelo Press, 2003). His first novel, *Suckerpunch*, will be published by HarperCollins in 2008. His poems have appeared in *FIELD*, *Ploughshares*, *The Missouri Review*, *TriQuarterly*, *AGNI*, *The Southern Review*, and *The Iowa Review*.

William Heyen's books include *Shoah Train: Poems* (Etruscan Press, 2003), which was a finalist for the National Book Award, *Crazy Horse in Stillness* (BOA Editions, 1996), winner of the Small Press Book Award, *Ribbons: The Gulf War* (Time Being Books, 1991), and *Erika: Poems of the Holocaust* (Vanguard Press, 1984). He is professor of English and poet-in-residence emeritus at the State University of New York at Brockport. He has won fellowships from the Guggenheim Foundation, the National Endowment for the Arts, and the American Academy of Arts and Letters.

Edward Hirsch has published six books of poetry: *Lay Back the Darkness* (2003), *On Love* (1998), *Earthly Measures* (1994), *The Night Parade* (1989), *Wild Gratitude* (1986), and *For the Sleepwalkers* (1981) (all from Alfred A. Knopf). He is president of the Guggenheim Foundation.

Daniel Hoffman served as Poet Laureate of the United States in 1973–74, an appointment then termed Consultant in Poetry to the Library of Congress. His many books include *Makes You Stop and Think: Sonnets* (George Braziller, 2005) and *Beyond Silence: Selected Shorter Poems, 1948–2003* (Louisiana State University Press, 2003).

Cynthia Huntington is the author of three volumes of poetry, *The Radiant* (Four Way Books, 2003), *We Have Gone to the Beach* (Alice James Books, 1996), and *The Fish-Wife* (University of Hawai'i Press, 1986), and a prose memoir, *The Salt House: A Summer on the Dunes of Cape Cod* (University Press of New England, 1999). A professor of English at Dartmouth College, she also teaches in the MFA Writing Program at Vermont College.

David Ignatow (1914–97) published seventeen books of poetry and received the Bollingen Prize, two Guggenheim Fellowships, and a National Institute of Arts and Letters award. He taught at York College/CUNY and at Columbia University.

Lawson Fusao Inada, a third-generation Japanese American who spent his early childhood in concentration camps in California, Arkansas, and Colorado, is emeritus professor of English at Southern Oregon State University. His books of poetry include *Drawing the Line* (Coffee House Press, 1997), *Legends from Camp* (Coffee House Press, 1993), and *Before the War* (Morrow, 1971). His honors include an American Book Award and fellowships from the National Endowment for the Arts and the Guggenheim Foundation.

Brigit Kelly has published three books of poetry: *The Orchard* (BOA Editions, 2004), *Song* (BOA Editions, 1995), and *To the Place of Trumpets* (Yale University Press, 1987), winner of the Yale Series of Younger Poets prize. Her work has appeared in many anthologies and literary magazines, including *The Nation*, *The Yale Review*, *Poetry*, and *The Antioch Review*.

Jane Kenyon (1947–95) published four volumes of poetry during her lifetime. Graywolf Press issued two posthumous works, *Collected Poems* (2005) and *A Hundred White Daffodils* (1999). She lived in New Hampshire with her husband, Donald Hall, until her death.

Peter Klappert is the author of six books of poetry. *The Idiot Princess of the Last Dynasty* will be reprinted in the Carnegie Mellon Classic Contemporary poetry series, and *Chokecherries: New and Selected Poems, 1966–1999* appeared in 2000 from Orchises Press. He has taught at Rollins College, Harvard University, the New College of Florida, the College of William and Mary, and George Mason University.

Richard Krawiec is the author of two novels, *Time Sharing* (Viking Press, 1986) and *Faith in What?* (Avisson Press, 1996), as well as a collection of short stories, *And Fools of God* (Avisson Press, 2000). His poetry appears in many literary magazines. He has been awarded fellowships from the National Endowment for the Arts, the North Carolina Arts Council, and the Pennsylvania Council on the Arts.

Carol Lem's books include *Shadow of the Plum* (Cedar Hill Publications, 2002), *The Hermit's Journey: Tarot Poems for Meditation* (Peddlar Press, 1993), *Don't Ask Why* (Peddlar Press, 1982), *Grassroots* (Peddlar Press, 1975), and *Searchings* (Vantage Press, 1971). Her poems have appeared in numerous journals, including *The Asian Pacific American Journal*, *The Bloomsbury Review*, *Blue Mesa Review*, *The Illinois Review*, *Many Mountains Moving*, *Rattle*, *The Seattle Review*, and *Yankee Magazine*.

Jean Lenski (1928–94) was the author of *The Molten Sea* (1996), a collection of poems published posthumously by Overmountain Press, and *Genesis: The Poetry of Jean Lenski* (St. Andrews College Press, 1993).

Rika Lesser is the author of *All We Need of Hell* (University of North Texas Press, 1995), *Growing Back: Poems, 1972–1992* (University of South Carolina Press), and *Etruscan Things* (George Braziller, 1983). She has translated several volumes of verse, among them Gunnar Ekelöf's *Guide to the Underworld*, *Rilke: Between Roots*, and *A Child Is Not a Knife: Selected Poems of Göran Sonnevi*.

Robert J. Levy is the author of six books of poetry, including *In the Century of Small Gestures* (Defined Providence Press, 2000). His poems have been published in *Poetry*, *The Paris Review*, *The Kenyon Review*, *The Georgia Review*, and *The Southern Review*.

Lyn Lifshin is the author of more than one hundred books and chapbooks. Black Sparrow Press published two volumes of her selected poems, *Cold Comfort* (1997) and *Before It's Light* (1999). She has also edited several anthologies of women's writing, including *Lips Unsealed* (Capra Press, 1990), *Ariadne's Thread* (Harper & Row, 1982), and *Tangled Vines* (Beacon Press, 1978).

Gregory Luce received a BA in English and an MA in creative writing from Oklahoma State University and did additional graduate work in writing at the University of Southern Mississippi. He has published poems and articles in numerous journals in the United States, Canada, and Great Britain. He lives in Washington, D.C.

Susan Ludvigson's books of poetry include *Sweet Confluence: New and Selected Poems* (Louisiana State University Press, 2000) and *Escaping the House of Certainty* (Louisiana State University Press, 2006). She teaches at Winthrop University, in Rock Hill, South Carolina.

Paul Mariani's most recent books include *Deaths and Transfigurations: Poems* (Paraclete Press, 2005) and *Thirty Days: On Retreat with the Spiritual Exercises of Ignatius Loyola* (Viking Press, 2002).

William Matthews (1942–97) was born in Cincinnati, was educated at Yale and the University of North Carolina, and lectured all over the United States. His many books include *Search Party: Collected Poems* (Houghton Mifflin, 2004), and *Time and Money* (Houghton Mifflin, 1995), which won the National Book Critics Circle Award.

Peter Meinke has published seven books in the Pitt Poetry Series, most recently *The Contracted Word* (2006), *Zinc Fingers* (2001), and *Scars* (1996). His collection of stories, *Unheard Music*, and his book about writing, *The Shape of Poetry*, were published by Jefferson Press in 2007.

Robert Mezey is retired from Pomona College, where he was poet-in-residence and professor of English for twenty-three years. He has published many books, including volumes of verse, anthologies, and translations. His collected poems appeared from the University of Arkansas Press in 2000.

Alan Naslund is the author of the collection *Silk Weather* (Fleur-de-Lis Press, 1999). His poems have been published in *Pleiades*, *The Louisville Review*, and the *Abiko Annual*, and his essays, fiction, and drama have appeared in a variety of publications in the United States and Asia.

Leonard Nathan (1924–2007) was the author of seventeen volumes of poetry, including *Restarting the World* (2006), *Tears of the Old Magician* (2003), and *The Potato Eaters* (all from Orchises Press). He was professor emeritus of rhetoric at the University of California at Berkeley.

Nina Nyhart's two books of poetry are *Openers* (1979) and *French for Soldiers* (1987), both from Alice James Books. Her poems have appeared in *Poetry*, *FIELD*, *Sentence*, the *Tampa Review*, and *The Prose Poem: An International Journal*.

Joyce Carol Oates is a recipient of the National Book Award and the PEN/Malamud Award for Excellence in Short Fiction. Among her many books of fiction are the best sellers *The Falls* (Ecco Press, 2004), *Blonde* (Ecco Press, 2000), and *We Were the Mulvaneys* (Dutton, 1996). Her books of poetry include *Tenderness* (Ontario Review Press, 1996) and *The Time Traveler* (Dutton, 1989). She teaches at Princeton University.

Suzanne Paola is the author of four volumes of poetry, including *The Lives of the Saints* (University of Washington Press, 2002), which was a finalist for the Lenore Marshall Award, and *Bardo* (University of Wisconsin Press, 1998). Her nonfiction includes *A Mind Apart: Travels Through a Neurodiverse World* (Penguin, 2005) and *Body Toxic: An Environmental Memoir* (Counterpoint, 2001), written under the pen name Susanne Antonetta.

Linda Pastan's most recent book is *Queen of a Rainy Country* (W. W. Norton, 2006). *Carnival Evening: New and Selected Poems, 1968–1998* (W. W. Norton, 1998) was a finalist for the National Book Award. In 2003 she won the Ruth Lilly Prize and from 1991 to 1994 served as Poet Laureate of Maryland.

Michael Pettit's most recent book is *Riding for the Brand* (University of Oklahoma Press, 2006). He is the editor of *The Writing Path* (University of Iowa Press, 1995, 1996), a two-volume collection of poetry and prose drawn from writers' conferences, and the author of *Cardinal Points* (University of Iowa Press, 1988), winner of the Iowa Poetry Prize. He has received a National Endowment for the Arts Fellowship.

Robert Pinsky served three terms as Poet Laureate of the United States. His most recent books are *An Invitation to Poetry* (W. W. Norton, 2004), an anthology based on his Favorite Poem Project, and *Jersey Rain* (Farrar, Straus and Giroux, 2000).

Marjorie Power's latest book of poetry is *Flying on One Wing: Poems for Breast Cancer Patients and Survivors, and Those Who Love Them* (Samaritan Health Services, 2006). Her other books are *Cave Poems* (1998) and *Tishku, After She Created Men* (1996), both published by Lone Willow Press.

Alberto Alvaro Ríos is the author of nine books and chapbooks of poetry, three collections of short stories, and a memoir. His books of poetry include, most recently, *The Theater of Night* (Copper Canyon Press, 2005) and *The Smallest Muscle in the Human Body* (Copper Canyon Press, 2002), which was a finalist for the National Book Award.

Elspeth Cameron Ritchie is a psychiatrist and a colonel in the United States Army, stationed in the Office of the Army Surgeon General. Both her scientific articles and her poems have been published widely. She is also the co-editor of a textbook, *Interventions Following Mass Violence and Disaster: Strategies for Mental Health Practice*, published in 2006 by Guilford Press.

Alane Rollings has published five collections of poetry: *To Be in This Number* (TriQuarterly Books, 2005), *The Logic of Opposites* (TriQuarterly Books, 1998), *The Struggle to Adore* (Story Line Press, 1994), *In Your Own Sweet Time* (Wesleyan University Press, 1989), and *Transparent Landscapes* (Raccoon Books, 1984).

Liz Rosenberg is the author of three volumes of poetry and numerous books and anthologies for children. She teaches at the State University of New York at Binghamton.

Vern Rutsala's *How We Spent Our Time* (University of Akron Press, 2006) won the Akron Poetry Prize. His other books are *The Moment's Equation* (Ashland Poetry Press, 2004), which was a finalist for the National Book Award, *Little-Known Sports* (University of Massachusetts Press, 1994), winner of the Juniper Prize, and *Selected Poems* (Story Line Press, 1991), winner of the Oregon Book Award.

Ira Sadoff is the author of seven books of poetry, most recently *Barter* (2003) and *Grazing* (1998) (both from the University of Illinois Press), and *An Ira Sadoff Reader* (University Press of New England, 1992). He teaches at Colby College, in Waterville, Maine, and in the MFA program at New England College.

Reg Saner's poetry has won the Walt Whitman Award, presented by the Academy of American Poets, and a National Poetry Series Open Competition award, and he has held a fellowship from the National Endowment for the Arts. His most recent book is a work of nonfiction on the American West, *The Dawn Collector* (Center for American Places, 2005).

Cheryl Savageau's third book of poems is *Mother/Land* (2006), published in Salt Publishing's Earthworks series. She has received fellowships in poetry from the National Endowment for the Arts and the Massachusetts Artists Foundation. Her poems have appeared in *AGNI*, the *Boston Review*, the *Indiana Review*, and other literary journals.

Harvey Shapiro is the author of eleven books of poetry, the most recent of which is *The Sights Along the Harbor: New and Collected Poems* (Wesleyan University Press, 2006). He is a Rockefeller grantee and a Pushcart Prize winner.

Enid Shomer is the author of four books of poetry, including *Black Drum* (University of Arkansas Press, 1997), and two collections of short stories, *Tourist Season* (Random House, 2007) and *Imaginary Men* (University of Iowa Press, 1993). Her poems and stories have appeared in *The New Yorker*, *The Atlantic*, *The Paris Review*, *Best American Poetry*, and *Poetry*.

Marcia Southwick's most recent book of poetry is *A Saturday Night at the Flying Dog* (Oberlin College Press, 1999), which won the 1998 FIELD Poetry Prize. She lives in Santa Fe, New Mexico.

Brian Swann has published many volumes of poetry, short fiction, and translations, in addition to books for children. The editor of a number of volumes on Native American literatures, he teaches at Cooper Union.

Donna Trussell lives in Kansas City, Missouri. Her fiction and poems have appeared in the *North American Review*, *TriQuarterly*, and *Poetry*. Her essays have appeared in *Newsweek* and the *Kansas City Star*.

Pamela Uschuk is the author of four books of poetry: *Without the Comfort of Stars: New and Selected Poems* (Sampark Press, 2007), *Scattered Risks* (Wings Press, 2005), *One-Legged Dancer* (Wings Press, 2002), and *Finding Peaches in the Desert* (Wings Press, 2000). She teaches creative writing at Fort Lewis College, in Durango, Colorado, and edits *Cutthroat: A Journal of the Arts*.

Patricia Vermillion lives in Hampton, Virginia, and teaches poetry for Christopher Newport University's Lifelong Learning Society. Her poems have appeared in the *Black Bear Review* and *Nimrod International*, among other journals.

Tino Villanueva is the author of five collections of poetry, including *Shaking Off the Dark* (Arte Publico Press, 1984; new edition, Bilingual Review Press, 1998), *Chronicle of My Worst Years* (TriQuarterly Books, 1994), and *Scene from the Movie GIANT* (Curbstone, 1993), which won a 1994 American Book Award. He teaches at Boston University.

Belle Waring's books of poetry include *Dark Blonde* (Sarabande, 1997) and *Refuge* (University of Pittsburgh Press, 1990). She has received fellowships from the National Endowment for the Arts and from the Fine Arts Work Center in Provincetown, Massachusetts.

C. K. Williams's books of poetry include *Collected Poems* (Farrar, Straus and Giroux, 2006), *Repair* (Farrar, Straus and Giroux, 1999), for which he won the Pulitzer Prize, and *The Singing* (Farrar, Straus and Giroux, 2003), winner of the National Book Award. He teaches in the writing program at Princeton University.

Miller Williams is the author of several volumes of poems, including *Some Jazz a While* (University of Illinois Press, 1999), and a collection of short stories, *The Lives of Kelvin Fletcher* (University of Georgia Press, 2002), as well as *Making a Poem: Some Thoughts About*

Poetry and the People Who Write It (Louisiana State University Press, 2006). "A Little Poem" is dedicated to Jack Marr.

David Wojahn is the author of six books of poetry, including *Interrogation Palace: New and Selected Poems 1982–2004* (University of Pittsburgh Press, 2006) and *Icehouse Lights* (Yale University Press, 1982), winner of the Yale Series of Younger Poets prize. The recipient of fellowships from the Guggenheim Foundation and the National Endowment for the Arts, he teaches at Virginia Commonwealth University and in the MFA Writing Program at Vermont College.

Jeffrey Zable has been a teacher for twenty-five years. He plays conga for Afro-Cuban dance classes, and his poetry and prose have appeared in many magazines and anthologies.

ACKNOWLEDGMENTS

INTRODUCTION

Quotations from Denise Levertov are from "Anne Sexton: Light Up the Cave," by Denise Levertov, from *Light Up The Cave*, copyright © 1981 by New Directions Publishing Corporation. Reprinted by permission of New Directions Publishing Corporation.

The quotation from Edwin Muir is reprinted by permission of the publishers from *The Estate of Poetry*, by Edwin Muir, p. 81, Cambridge, Mass.: Harvard University Press, copyright © 1962 by the President and Fellows of Harvard College.

The quotation from William Stafford is from *The Writer's Mind: Interviews with American Authors*, copyright © 1989 by Irv Broughton. Reprinted by permission of the University of Arkansas Press, www.uapress.com.

POEMS

Sandra Agricola: "Paperweight: The State I'm In," copyright © 1995 by Sandra Agricola. A version of "Paperweight: The State I'm In" appears in "Problem of Blue," from *Yellow* (Mercy Seat Press), by Sandra Agricola. Copyright © 2004 by Sandra Agricola. Used by permission of the author.

Dick Allen: "A Lonely Stretch of Road," copyright © 2007 by Dick Allen. Used by permission of the author.

David Baker: "Bedlam," from *Midwest Eclogue*, by David Baker. Copyright © 2005 by David Baker. Used by permission of W. W. Norton & Company, Inc.

Leo Connellan: "Helpless We Go Into This Ground, Helpless," from *Another Poet in New York* (Living Poets Press), by Leon Connellan. Copyright © 1975 by Leo Connellan. Reprinted by permission of the author and the Estate of Leo Connellan.

Peter Cooley: "In the Crepuscular," from *Nightseasons* (Carnegie Mellon University Press), by Peter Cooley. Copyright © 1983 by Peter Cooley. "Irises" and "The Enclosed Field," from *The Van Gogh Notebook* (Carnegie Mellon University Press), by Peter Cooley. Copyright © 1987 by Peter Cooley. "Returning from the Shopping Center to the Suburbs," from *The Company of Strangers* (University of Missouri Press), by Peter Cooley. Copyright © 1975 by Peter Cooley. All reprinted by permission of the author.

Sheila Cowing: "Vegetable Garden After Too Much Rain," from *Stronger in the Broken Places*, by Sheila Cowing. Copyright © 1999 by Sheila Cowing. Reprinted by permission of Sherman Asher Publishing and the author.

Steven Cramer: "Bipolar" is from *Goodbye to the Orchard*, by Steven Cramer, published by Sarabande Books, Inc., copyright © 2004 by Steven Cramer. Reprinted by permission of Sarabande Books and the author. "Thanksgiving," from *The Eye That Desires to Look Upward* (Galileo Press), copyright © 1987 by Steven Cramer. Reprinted by permission of the author.

Erica Dawson: "Disorder," from *Big-Eyed Afraid*, by Erica Dawson. Copyright © 2007 by Erica Dawson. Reprinted by permission of Waywiser Press (London and Baltimore).

Miriam Dyak: "Mania," copyright © 2007 by Miriam Dyak. Used by permission of the author.

Jane Flanders: "Stasis" is reprinted by permission of University of Massachusetts Press from *The Students of Snow*, by Jane Flanders, copyright © 1982 by Jane Flanders.

C. B. Follett: "Man on Fire," copyright © 1992 by CB Follett, first appeared in *Perception III*. Used by permission of the author.

Reginald Gibbons: "Analytical Episodes" and "Question," from *Maybe It Was So* (University of Chicago Press), by Reginald Gibbons. Copyright © 1991 by Reginald Gibbons. Reprinted by permission of the author.

Edward Hirsch: "Christopher Smart," from *For the Sleepwalker* (Carnegie Mellon University Press), by Edward Hirsch. Copyright © 1998 by Edward Hirsch. Reprinted by permission of the author.

Daniel Hoffman: "A Dreamer" reprinted by permission of Louisiana State University Press from *Beyond Silence: Selected Shorter Poems, 1948–2003*, by Daniel Hoffman. Copyright © 2003 by Daniel Hoffman.

Cynthia Huntington: "There," from *The Fish-Wife* (University of Hawai'i Press), by Cynthia Huntington. Copyright © 1986 by Cynthia Huntington. Reprinted by permission of the author.

David Ignatow: "Spinning," "Holes I want to creep into," "I must make my own sun . . . ," and "I'm Sure," by David Ignatow, from *New and Collected Poems, 1970–1985* (Wesleyan University Press, 1986). Copyright © 1986 by David Ignatow and reprinted by permission of Wesleyan University Press. "Figures of the Human," by David Ignatow, from *Against the Evidence: Selected Poems, 1934–1994* (Wesleyan University Press, 1993). Copyright © 1993 by David Ignatow and reprinted by permission of Wesleyan University Press.

Lawson Fusao Inada: "Don't Know," from *Before the War* (Morrow), by Lawson Fusao Inada. Copyright © 1971 by Lawson Fusao Inada. Reprinted by permission of the author.

Brigit Kelly: "Figure of Distress in a Field," copyright © 1990 by Brigit Kelly, first appeared in *Creeping Bent*. Reprinted by permission of the author.

Jane Kenyon: "In the Grove: The Poet at Ten," "Depression in Winter," "Having It Out with Melancholy," and "Happiness" copyright © 2005 by the Estate of Jane Kenyon. Reprinted from *Collected Poems* with the permission of Graywolf Press, Saint Paul, Minnesota.

Peter Klappert: "This," from *Chokecherries: New and Selected Poems, 1966–1999* (Orchises Press), by Peter Klappert. Copyright © 2000 by Peter Klappert. Reprinted by permission of the author.

Richard Krawiec: "God's Face," copyright © 1995 by Richard Krawiec. Used by permission of the author.

Carol Lem: "Something Is There," from *Shadow of the Plum* (Cedar Hill Publications), by Carol Lem. Copyright © 2002 by Carol Lem. Used by permission of the author.

Jean Lenski: "Explanation," from *Genesis* (St. Andrews Press), by Jean Lenski. Copyright © 1993 by Jean Lenski. Reprinted by permission of the author and Gerhard Lenski.

Rika Lesser: "On Lithium: After One Year / After Two," from Rika Lesser, *All We Need of Hell* (University of North Texas Press, 1995), copyright © 1995 Rika Lesser. Reprinted by permission of the author and the University of North Texas Press.

Robert J. Levy: "Meditation on Virginia Woolf's Final Diary Entry, Written Three Weeks Before Her Suicide," from *In the Century of Small Gestures* (Defined Providence Press), by Robert J. Levy. Copyright © 2000 by Robert J. Levy.

Lyn Lifshin: "depression" and "Depression," copyright © 1995 by Lyn Lifshin. Used by permission of the author.

Gregory Luce: "The animal night sweats of the spirits burn," copyright © 2007 by Gregory Luce. Used by permission of the author.

Susan Ludvigson: "Grief," from *The Swimmer* (Louisiana State University Press), by Susan Ludvigson. Copyright © 1984 by Susan Ludvigson. Reprinted by permission of the author.

Paul Mariani: "Mountain View with Figures," from *The Great Wheel*, by Paul Mariani. Copyright © 1996 by Paul Mariani. Used by permission of W. W. Norton & Company, Inc.

William Matthews: "Manic" and "Depressive," from *A Happy Childhood* (Little, Brown and Company), by William Matthews. Copyright © 1985 by William Matthews. Reprinted by permission of the Estate of William Matthews.

Peter Meinke: "The Poet to His Tongue," from *Liquid Paper: New and Selected Poems*, by Peter Meinke, copyright © 1991. Reprinted by permission of the University of Pittsburgh Press.

Robert Mezey: "No Country You Remember," from *Collected Poems: 1952–1999* (University of Arkansas Press), copyright © 2000 by Robert Mezey. Reprinted by permission of the author.

Alan Naslund: "Granary for Pop," copyright © 2007 by Alan Naslund. Used by permission of the author.

Leonard Nathan: "The Poet's House Preserved as a Museum," from *Carrying On: New and Selected Poems*, by Leonard Nathan, copyright © 1985. Reprinted by permission of the University of Pittsburgh Press.

Nina Nyhart: "Arrow," copyright © 1995 by Nina Nyhart, first appeared in *The Bridge*. Reprinted by permission of the author.

Joyce Carol Oates: "Mania: Early Phase," from *The Time Traveler*, by Joyce Carol Oates. Copyright © 1989 by Joyce Carol Oates. Reprinted by permission of Ontario Review, Inc.

Suzanne Paola: "Glass," from *Glass* (*Quarterly Review of Literature*, vol. 34), by Suzanne Paola. Copyright © 1995 by Suzanne Paola. Reprinted by permission of the author.

Linda Pastan: "Hurricane Watch," from *Aspects of Eve*, by Linda Pastan. Copyright © 1970, 1971, 1972, 1973, 1974, 1975 by Linda Pastan. Used by permission of Liveright Publishing Corporation.

Michael Pettit: "Fat Tuesday," copyright © 1995 by Michael Pettit, first appeared in the *Chariton Review*. Reprinted by permission of the author. "Bewildering Miracle," copyright © 2007 by Michael Pettit. Used by permission of the author.

Robert Pinsky: "Exile," from *The Want Bone*, by Robert Pinsky, copyright © 1990 by Robert Pinsky. Reprinted by permission of HarperCollins Publishers.

Marjorie Power: "*The Madwoman* by Picasso," copyright © 1995 by Marjorie Power, first appeared in *Word Outta Buffalo*. Reprinted by permission of the author.

Alberto Alvaro Ríos: "What She Had Believed All Her Life," from *Lime Orchard Woman: Poems* (Sheep Meadow Press), by Alberto Alvaro Ríos. Copyright © 1988 by Alberto Alvaro Ríos. Reprinted by permission of the author.

Elspeth Cameron Ritchie: "Spring Lettuce," copyright © 1990 by Elspeth Cameron Ritchie, first appeared in *The Radcliffe Quarterly*. Reprinted by permission of the author.

Alane Rollings: "The Logic of Opposites," from *The Logic of Opposites*, by Alane Rollings. Copyright © 1998 by Alane Rollings. Reprinted by permission of the author.

Liz Rosenberg: "New Days," from *Children of Paradise*, by Liz Rosenberg, copyright © 1994. Reprinted by permission of the University of Pittsburgh Press. "The Depression: Triple Haiku," copyright © 2003 by Liz Rosenberg, first appeared in the *Bellevue Literary Review*. Reprinted by permission of the author. "Fighting Despair: A Haiku Sequence," copyright © 1995 by Liz Rosenberg. Reprinted by permission of the author.

Vern Rutsala: "Against Telephones," copyright © 1995 by Vern Rutsala. Used by permission of the author.

Ira Sadoff: "Depression Beginning in 1965," from *Palm Reading in Winter*, by Ira Sadoff. Copyright © 1978 by Ira Sadoff. Reprinted by permission of the author.

Reg Saner: "Astrophysics," copyright © 1994 by Reg Saner, first appeared in *Ploughshares*. Reprinted by permission of the author.

Cheryl Savageau: "Thorns," by Cheryl Savageau, from *Dirt Road Home* (Curbstone Press, 1995). Reprinted with permission of Curbstone Press. Distributed by Consortium.

Harvey Shapiro: "Days and Nights," by Harvey Shapiro, from *The Sights Along the Harbor: New and Collected Poems* (Wesleyan University Press, 2006). Copyright © 2006 by Harvey Shapiro and reprinted by permission of Wesleyan University Press.

Enid Shomer: "My Friend Who Sings Before Breakfast," from *Black Drum*. Copyright © 1997 by Enid Shomer. Reprinted with the permission of the University of Arkansas Press, www.uapress.com.

Marcia Southwick: "The Mood Museum: *Anxiety*," "The Mood Museum: *Depression*," and "The Mood Museum: *Sloth & Torpor*," from *A Saturday Night at the Flying Dog*, by Marcia Southwick, Oberlin College Press, copyright © 1999. Reprinted by permission of Oberlin College Press. "Interiors" and "Born Again in a Moment of Amnesia," copyright © 2007 by Marcia Southwick. Used by permission of the author.

Brian Swann: "Bipolar" and "Circus Framework," copyright © 1995 by Brian Swann. Used by permission of the author.

Donna Trussell: "Snow," copyright © 1987 by Donna Trussell, first appeared in *Poetry Northwest*. Reprinted by permission of the author.

Pamela Uschuk: "To Play by Heart," copyright © 1984 by Pamela Uschuk, first appeared in *Zonë*. Reprinted by permission of the author.

Patricia Vermillion: "St. Dympna and St. Ottilia," copyright © 2005 by Patricia Vermillion, first appeared in *North Central Review* under the title "A Quiet Game." Reprinted by permission of the author.

Tino Villanueva: "Again," "Now, As We Drop: A Poem of Guilt," and "Shaking Off the Dark," from *Shaking Off the Dark* (Arte Público Press, 1984; Bilingual Press, 1998), copyright © 1984, 1998 by Tino Villanueva. Reprinted by permission of the author.

Belle Waring: "Bipolar Affective Disorder as Possible Adaptive Advantage," from *Dark Blonde*, by Belle Waring, published by Sarabande Books, Inc., copyright © 1997 by Belle Waring. Reprinted by permission of Sarabande Books and the author.

C. K. Williams: "Dominion: Depression," from *The Vigil*, by C. K. Williams. Copyright © 1997 by C. K. Williams. Reprinted by permission of Farrar, Straus and Giroux, LLC.

INDEX OF AUTHORS